MUSEUM KUNST PALAST
Ehrenhof 4-5
40479 Düsseldorf Germany

„COMING HOME"

HANDWOVEN OUTDOOR FURNITURE CREATED WITH WEATHER-RESISTANT DEDON FIBER

DEDON®

DEDON worldwide: www.dedon.de · office@dedon.de

Più

The new Occhio spotlight series.
With the first LED generation that
meets our demands.

Occhio lets people design their own lighting and living environment. The new Più unites the unique modularity and the simple inspirational design of Occhio in a multifunctional spotlight series.

With its Smart Source concept Più offers the right light source for every requirement in private and public spaces. The innovative, interchangeable high performance LED and latest halogen and metal halide technologies ensure the perfect balance between energy efficiency and maximum light quality. For quality of light means quality of life. Experience Più on our website **www.occhio-piu.com**

AR – Augmented Reality
Download ›Junaio‹ from the App Store free of charge onto your smartphone. Select the Occhio Più channel, hold your smartphone over the product illustration or the studio image and experience Occhio Più.

light is evolution

Occhio

kvadrat

Graphic Thought Facility   Photography: Matthew Donaldson

diversity is the new paradigm in workplace design.

climate®
workclimate.com

climate®
a Schiavello initiative

the mosaic never seen

Free compositions to interpret and express ideas, personality and lifestyle through the geometry of mosaics.
The rich colour palette and tiny chips of Vetrina make it possible to recreate sophisticated textures and subtle nuances with photographic realism.

www.mosaicopiu.it

The art of less
UNDER-COVER
DOORFRAMES
www.under-cover-doorframes.com

LOUNGE CHAIR OTTO:
"I AM OPEN TO ALL DIRECTIONS AND ALL CONNECTIONS."
DESIGN CARLOS TISCAR

www.girsberger.com

girsberger

koelnmesse

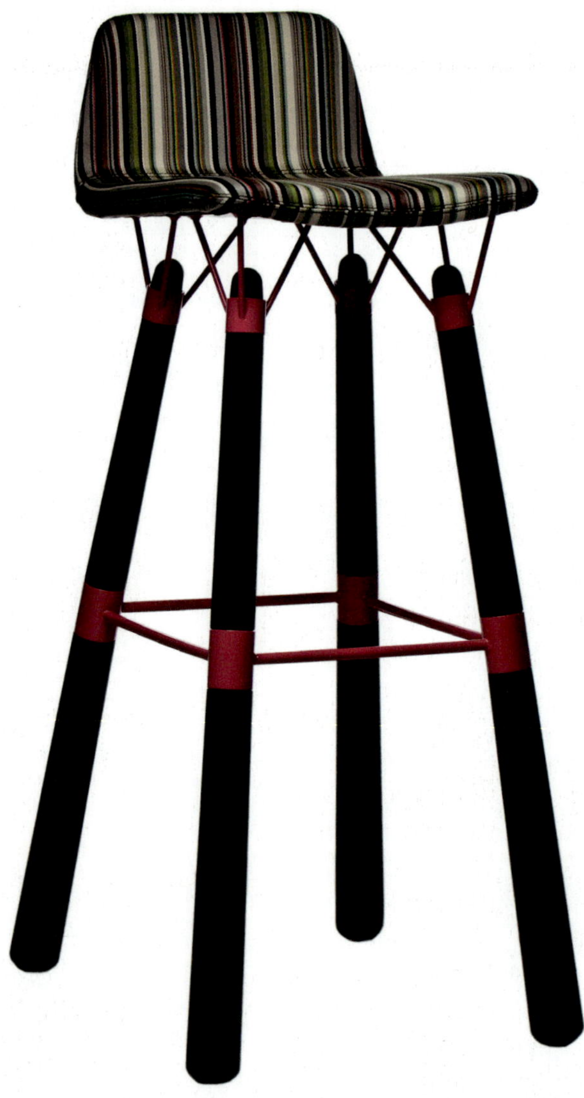

Nest Generation

The all new family of Nest from Johanson Design
Design by Alexander Lervik

WWW.JOHANSONDESIGN.SE

AD: Roberto Bandiera / PH. Lorenzo Vitturi
CERAMICHE REFIN
DEUS EX MACHINA
KAOS COLLECTION
design by Luca Nichetto

REFIN®
CERAMICHE
WWW.REFIN.IT

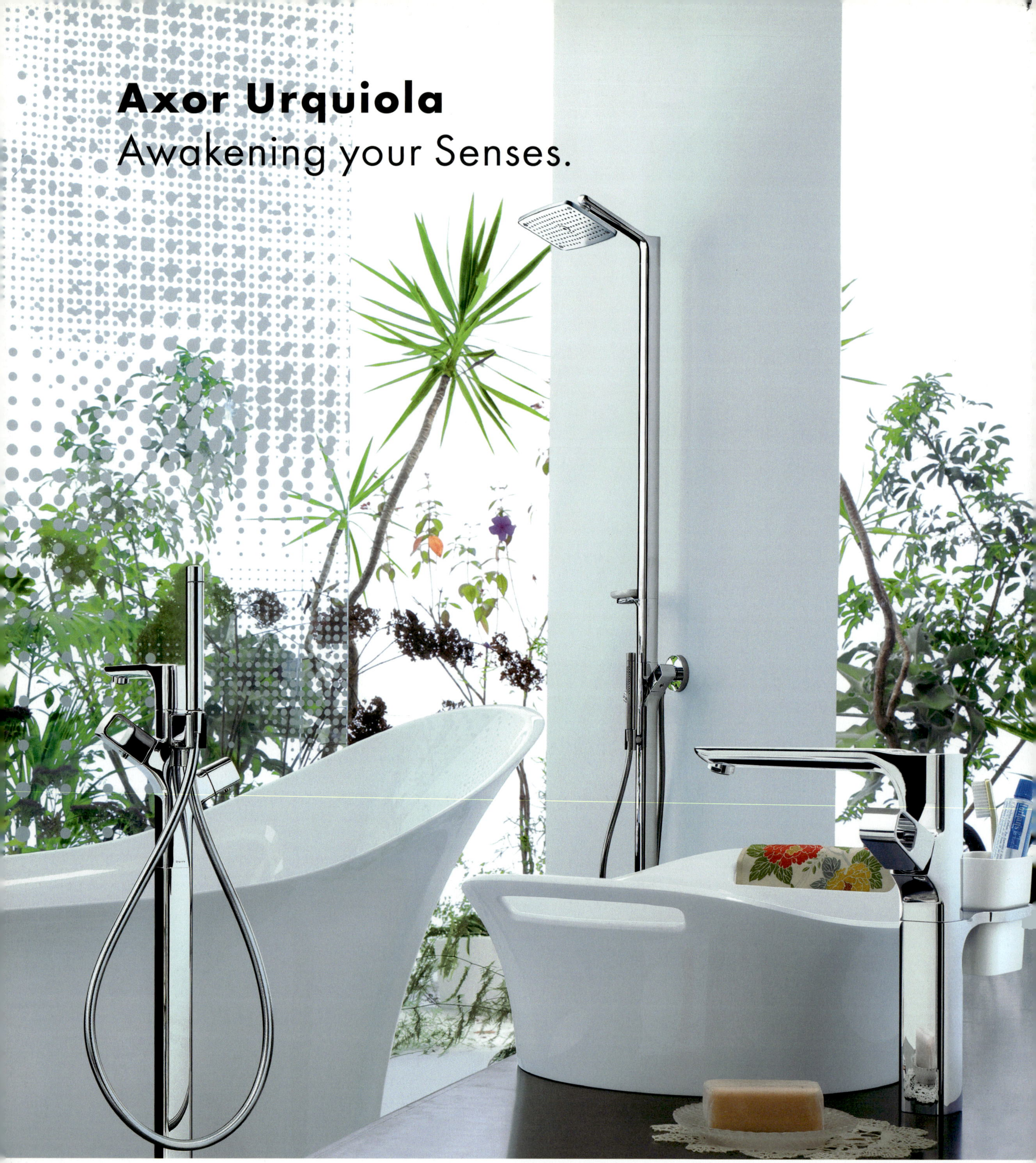

Axor Urquiola
Awakening your Senses.

Visit **www.axor-design.com** for more information on the Axor Urquiola bathroom collection and the designer Patricia Urquiola.

Xair

Inspiring Decisions and Productivity

When the time comes to change the world,
Xair is there to support the decision making.
The feeling of support you get from the chair
wrapping your entire body, and the sense of security you
get from being able to entrust your body to the chair.
The Xair offers the best seating position for all occasions,
supporting important business situations by inducing
creativity and vitality.
Think of it as a reliable business partner.

Designed by Ken Okuyama

PLAN@OFFICE
Van Zandvlietplein 19
3077 AA ROTTERDAM
www.planatoffice.nl

Inaba
www.inaba-ss.co.jp

BRIGHT
BRIGHT stuff by
WALOO LEE
BRIGHT
Vol van vernieuwing
Subscribe now and get free artwork
BRIGHT
Vol van vernieuwing
subscribe at
www.bright.nl

→FLAMINIA.
foto: f. faedda studio21
ceramicaflaminia.it

Barrisol® Lumière®
MaXXI Museum - Roma - Italy
by Zaha Hadid

Crédit photo Zaha Hadid Architects © 2009
photographer : Roland Halbe

These exceptional projects
have one thing in common

BARRISOL®
WORLD LEADER OF STRETCHED CEILING

Barrisol® Origami Tigers
Sydney - Australia
by LAVA Architects

Barrisol® Acoustics®
Opera House - Oslo - Norway
by Snohetta Architects
2009 European Award
of Contemporary Architecture

Barrisol®
Mediacite Shopping Center
Liege - Belgium
by Ron Arad
& Jaspers-Eyers architects

www.barrisol.com

THERE IS LIGHT ON EARTH.

La scuola

Cosmic Leaf, design Ross Lovegrove.

Artemide turns on a light for Aung San Suu Kyi, Nobel Peace Prize in 1991.
Years and years spent in the darkness of tyranny in Burma,
living her life under the guiding light of non-violence.
Compensation will be entirely donated to the Burmese Exile Government.

Artemide®
THE HUMAN LIGHT.

www.artemide.com Tel. 020 76315200

Toot sofa by Piero Lissoni and Cassina. Design first.

Lissoni's elegant design combined with the skilled craftsmanship of Cassina come together to bring you Toot. A modular system with an aluminium frame, feather padding and a choice of seat depths allowing many different permutations. Available with or without armrests and with or without back cushions, you will always feel at home with Toot. www.cassina.com

Cassina

IA+B, PAGE 116.

FEATURES
PROJECTS IN PERSPECTIVE

FREELAND BUCK, PAGE 154.

DATA NATURE, PAGE 050.

EERO AARNIO, PAGE 212.

GAMFRATESI, PAGE 194.

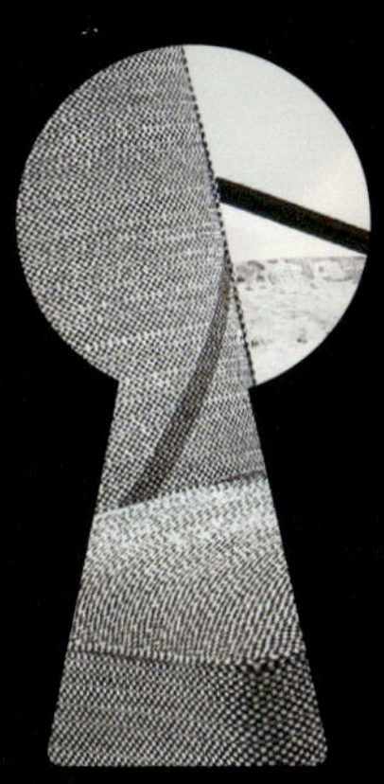

heimtextil-trends.com

FRAME
Laan der Hesperiden 68
NL-1076 DX Amsterdam
T +31 20 423 3717
F +31 20 428 0653
info@framemag.com
framemag.com

EDITORIAL
editorial@framemag.com

EDITOR IN CHIEF
Robert Thiemann

MANAGING EDITOR
Femke de Wild

EDITORS
Tracey Ingram
Jane Szita

EDITORIAL INTERN
Cassandra Pizzey

CONTRIBUTING EDITORS
Shonquis Moreno
Alexandra Onderwater
Louise Schouwenberg
Chris Scott
Michael Webb

COPY EDITOR
Donna de Vries-Hermansader

ART DIRECTION
Roelof Mulder

GRAPHIC DESIGN
Mariëlle van Genderen
Cathelijn Kruunenberg
Adriaan Mellegers
Marco Ugolini

TRANSLATION
InOtherWords
(Donna de Vries-Hermansader)

**CONTRIBUTORS TO
THIS ISSUE**
Giovanna Dunmall
Grant Gibson
Daniel Golling
Cathelijne Nuijsink
Rick Poynor
Anna Sansom
Matthew Stewart
Masaaki Takahashi
Charlotte Vaudrey
Suzanne Wales

WEB EDITOR
Marc Klis
marc@framemag.com

COVER
Designed by Roelof Mulder
Photo Courtesy of
2012Architecten

LITHOGRAPHY
Edward de Nijs

PRINTING
Grafisch Bedrijf Tuijtel,
Hardinxveld-Giessendam

PAPER
280gr Trucard Linen, 135gr
Sappi Mat, 115gr Hello Gloss
and 100gr IJsselprint

PUBLISHER
Peter Huiberts
peter@framemag.com

DISTRIBUTION
Benjamin Verheijden
benjamin@framemag.com

FINANCE
Sandy Kenswil
sandy@framemag.com

**MARKETING AND
COMMUNICATION**
Fee Pfeiffer
fee@framemag.com

ADVERTISING
Elles Middeljans
elles@framemag.com
Michal Kislev-Reshef
michal@framemag.com

**ADVERTISING
REPRESENTATIVES
AUSTRIA/GERMANY/
SWITZERLAND**
Xenia Lange
Wolfram Werbung
Feringastrasse 9a
D-85774 Unterfoehring
T +49 89 992 493 990
F +49 89 992 493 999
wolframwerbung.com
lange@wolframwerbung.com
wolfram@wolframwerbung.com

ITALY
Studio Mitos
Michele Tosato
Via Valdrigo 40
I-31048 San Biagio di Callalta
(TV)
T +39 0422 894 868
F +39 0422 895 634
studio.mitos@tin.it

SPAIN
Publistar
Vibeke Gilland
Cea Bermúdez 10, Ático
ES-Madrid 28003
T +34 91 553 4206
F +34 91 554 4664
M +34 60 761 3111
vibeke.gilland@publistar-es.com

UNITED KINGDOM
Francine Libessart
T +44 20 7704 0944
francine@framemag.com

**LICENSE HOLDERS
CHINA**
Frame China
Jacky Liu Zhanhui
T +86 411 8437 6131
jackyl@archi-china.com

RUSSIA
Mediacrat
Alexei Medvedev
T +7 495 627 7841
info@mediacrat.eu

TURKEY
Tibet Publishing Group Ltd.
Enis Tibet
T +90 21 2296 6758
info@framedergisi.com

SUBSCRIPTIONS
subscriptions@framemag.com
framemag.com

**SUBSCRIPTION
REPRESENTATIVES
JAPAN**
Memex Inc.
4-9-8 Minamisenba, Chuo-ku
JP-542-0081 Osaka
T +81 6 6281 2828
F +81 6 6258 4440
info@memex.ne.jp
memex.ne.jp

KOREA
Le Book/Beatboy
Baegang Building,
Kangnam-gu Shinsa-dong
666-11
KR-135-897 Seoul
T +82 11 746 4862
yourbeatboy@hanmail.net

SINGAPORE
Basheer Graphic Books
Block 231 Bain Street #04-19,
Bras Basah Complex
SG-180231 Singapore
T +65 6336 0810
F +65 6334 1950
bgbooks@singnet.com.sg

SUBSCRIPTION RATES
1-year €95
2-year €180
1-year student €85
2-year student €160

HOW TO SUBSCRIBE?
Visit framemag.com or
telephone +31 20 423 3717.

FRAME (USPS No: 019-372) is
published bimonthly by FRAME
Publishers and distributed in
the USA by DSW, 75 Aberdeen
Road, Emigsville, PA 17318.
Periodicals postage paid at
Emigsville, PA. POSTMASTER:
send address changes to
FRAME, c/o PO Box 437,
Emigsville, PA 17318-0437.

**BOOKSTORE DISTRIBUTORS
AUSTRALIA**
Speedimpex Australia Pty Ltd
T +61 2 9371 8866
F +61 2 9371 8867
sales@selectair.com.au

AUSTRIA
Morawa Pressevertrieb
T +43 1 5156 2190
F +43 1 5156 2881 955
mbaburek@morawa.com

BELGIUM
IMAPress
T +32 14 423 838
F +32 14 423 163
info@imapress.be

Exhibitions International
T +32 16 296 900
F +32 16 296 129
info@exhibitionsinternational.be

BRAZIL
Livraria Freebook
T +55 11 3256 0577
F +55 11 3259 1120
info@freebook.com.br

CANADA
LMPI
T +1 514 355 5674
mcoutu@lmpi.com

CHINA
Frame China
Jacky Liu Zhanhui
T +86 411 8437 6131
jackyl@archi-china.com

CYPRUS
Nasis Ltd.
T +357 9624 3125
niki@nasisbooks.com

DENMARK
Interpress Danmark
T +45 3327 7744
F +45 3327 7701
rr@interpressdanmark.dk

DUBAI
Tawseel Distribution
T +971 4344 2222
info@tawseel.com

FINLAND
Akateeminen Kirjakauppa
T +358 9 121 4330
F +358 9 121 4241
juha.kaski@stockmann.fi

FRANCE
OFR Systems International
T +33 1 4245 7288
F +33 1 4018 3978
info@ofrpublications.com

GERMANY
IPS Pressevertrieb
T +49 2225 8801 182
F +49 2225 8801 59182
lstulin@ips-d.de

Vice Versa Vertrieb
T +49 3061 6092 36
F +49 3061 6092 38
info@vice-versa-vertrieb.de

GREECE
Papasotiriou Bookstores
T +30 10 332 3306
F +30 10 384 8254
diamantopoulos
papasotiriou.gr

HONG KONG
The Grand Commercial Co., Ltd.
T +852 2 570 9639
F +852 2 570 4665
thegrandcc@i-cable.com

HUNGARY
IPS Pressevertrieb
T +49 2225 8801 182
F +49 2225 8801 59182
lstulin@ips-d.de

INDIA
SBD Subscription Services
T +91 11 2871 4138
F +91 11 2871 2268
sbds@bol.net.in

INDONESIA
Basheer Graphic Books
T +62 21 720 9151
F +62 21 720 9151
info@basheergraphic.com

ITALY
Idea Books SRL
T +39 0445 576 574
F +39 0445 577 764
info@ideabooks.it

JAPAN
Memex
T +81 6 6281 2828
F +81 6 6258 4440
info@memex.ne.jp

KOREA
Le Book/Beatboy
T +82 11 746 4862
yourbeatboy@hanmail.net

MALAYSIA
Basheer Graphic Books
T +603 2713 2236
F +603 2143 2236
info@basheergraphic.com

MALTA
Miller Distributors Ltd.
T +356 2166 4488
info@millermalta.com

MIDDLE EAST
AA Studio
T +961 1 990 199
F +961 1 990 188
aastudio@inco.com.lb

NETHERLANDS
Betapress
T +31 16 145 7800
F +31 16 145 3161
m.maican@betapress.audax.nl

NEW ZEALAND
Mag Nation Auckland
T +64 9366 6216
info@magnation.com

NORWAY
Listo AB
T +46 8 792 4668
carola.genas@listo.se

POLAND
IPS Pressevertrieb
T +49 2225 8801 182
F +49 2225 8801 59182
lstulin@ips-d.de

PORTUGAL
International News Portugal
T +351 21 898 2010
mario.dias@internews.com.pt

TEMA
T +351 21 342 4082
F +351 21 716 6925
belmiro@mail.telepac.pt

RUSSIA
Mediacrat
T +7 49 5228 4919
arman@mediacrat.ru

**SERBIA/BOSNIA &
HERZEGOVINA/MACEDONIA/
MONTENEGRO**
ARBOOKS d.o.o Beograd
T/F +381 11 242 7183
office@arbooks.net

SINGAPORE
Basheer Graphic Books
T +65 336 0810
F +65 334 1950
info@basheergraphic.com

SLOVAKIA
Art Books s.r.o.
T +421 25 2494 919
info@artbooks.sk

SOUTH AFRICA
Magscene
T +27 11 579 2000
F +27 11 579 2080
info@magscene.co.za

SPAIN
Promotora de Prensa
Internacional SA
T +34 93 245 1464
F +34 93 265 4883
evelazquez@promopress.es

SWEDEN
Svenska Interpress AB
T +46 8 5065 0615
F +46 8 5065 0750
susanne.pettersson
interpress.se

SWITZERLAND
IPS Pressevertrieb
T +49 2225 8801 182
F +49 2225 8801 59182
lstulin@ips-d.de

TAIWAN
Long Sea
T +886 2 2706 6838
F +886 2 2706 6109
eric@longsea.com.tw

TURKEY
Tasarim Publishing Group Ltd.
T +90 21 2296 6758
info@framedergisi.com

UNITED KINGDOM
Comag
T +44 20 1895 4337 33
F +44 20 1895 4336 03
louise.taylor@comag.co.uk

USA
Ubiquity Distributors
T +1 718 875 5491
F +1 718 875 8047
info@ubiquitymags.com

Comag
T +44 20 1895 4337 33
F +44 20 1895 4336 03
louise.taylor@comag.co.uk

a new vision: KELVIN LED
design by Antonio Citterio with Toan Nguyen
FLOS
Amsterdam, Cruquiusweg 109Q, +31 (0) 20 560 50 60
www.flos.com

CRITICAL? Yes.
It's time to tell the whole truth.

ENVIRONMENTAL
CLAIMS AND LABELS
CAN TELL PARTIAL
TRUTHS.

Sustainability is too complex
to be explained by a single
product benefit or green label.
We think customers should
have access to 3rd party certified
information about ingredients
and environmental impacts across
the full life cycle.

mission
Ø

Mission Zero:
our promise to eliminate
any negative impact our company
may have on the environment
by the year 2020.

www.interfaceflor.eu/letsbeclear

Interface FLOR

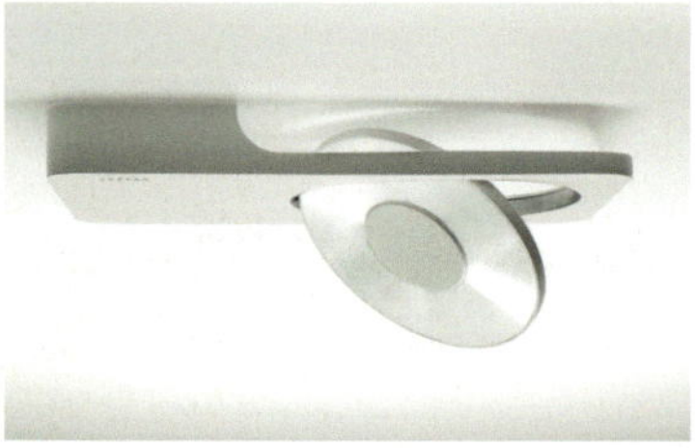

CAMPER
EXTRAOR DINARY CRAFTS
CREATIVE QUALITY & QUALITY EXECUTION

Camper Toðer
with Bernhard Willhelm.

Shop online at camper.com

"Wooden kitchen with technological heart"

"Noce Tattile" Artematica
Water-based varnish
No emissions of cancer-promoting aromatic solvents
The surfaces have a textured and warm feel
Very high stain resistance
Sustainably produced wood veneer finish

Invitrum base unit system
100% recyclable
100% glass and aluminium
100% mechanical fasteners
No formaldehyde emissions
Fully water-resistant
Easy to disassemble and reuse

Designed by Gabriele Centazzo   www.valcucine.com

VISIONS
FROM THE DRAWING BOARD

AN OVERSIZED BIRDCAGE IS THE CENTREPIECE OF THE LOBBY – A SPACE THAT ENGAGES ALL THE SENSES.

With their new venture CO, designer EDWARD VAN VLIET and hotel concept developer HANS MEYER focus on time and health to redefine luxury lodging in an ecologically responsible way.

WORDS **TRACEY INGRAM**
VISUALS **MICHIEL WIJNEN**

In the current ecological climate, green travel is becoming less of an added bonus and more of an expectation. While some hotels are making small changes, such as converting to energy-saving lamps and suggesting guests hang onto their towels for an extra day before they're washed, many customers just don't buy it. The initiatives seem like attempts to save the hotel money (also a result) rather than a dedicated sustainability effort, and often the experience isn't any better for the guest. Facing a sceptical audience, Studio Edward van Vliet (SEVV) and Hans Meyer (HotelsAhead and the initial creator of the modular CitizenM hotel concept) have developed CO – a location-inspired hotel concept that's all about taking time out and maintaining a healthy lifestyle. And, says Meyer, it 'just happens to be sustainable. Some existing "eco resorts" use

the term as a marketing technique,' he continues, 'and frequently the eco experience is not fused with the actual hotel experience.'

While eco-friendliness and sustainability are driving factors in the CO concept, they aren't the only issues, however. Meyer and Van Vliet believe the problem with hotel design is that many new projects are built according to a systematic plan which hasn't changed much over the years, and that new designs are in desperate need of differentiation from their ageing counterparts. You can walk into a chain hotel anywhere in the world and feel as though you've been there before, even if your last visit was to a same-name location thousands of kilometres away. Yet another factor is the current redefinition of luxury, which used to be about abundance but is now often associated with a

lack of pretension. 'In the future luxury will be synonymous with time and health, neither of which can really be bought,' says Meyer.

With health and relaxation in mind, Meyer and Van Vliet soon opted for a back-to-basics retreat – an 'oasis in the city' featuring a green courtyard at its centre: the hub of the hotel. Their next step was to 'build' space around the different points of contact – which are key to the CO brand – that confront guests prior to and during their stay at a hotel. Looking at the different elements, they saw how areas and facilities could be combined to reduce wasted or unused space.

'Breakfast is often served in one room, which is then vacant for the rest of the day,' explains Meyer. 'Our concept is made up of flexible spaces combined into one area.' For example, >>>

THE HOTEL WILL BE FURNISHED WITH NEWLY CUSTOM-MADE PIECES – CHARACTERIZED BY ECO FOAM AND UPHOLSTERY – INCLUDING THE SUSHI BLOCK SEAT (BELOW) FROM EDWARD VAN VLIET'S SUSHI COLLECTION, ORIGINALLY DESIGNED FOR MOROSO.

EACH CO HOTEL SHOULD HAVE A CHARACTER THAT'S TIED TO THE LOCATION: FUNDAMENTALLY THE SAME, BUT LOCALLY DIFFERENT.

instead of a reception desk and a shop, you could have a shop – offering local goods – with a counter where guests can also check into the hotel. From here, visitors enter the lobby, where CO attempts to engage all the senses. Digital art adds layers of sound, which is 'very subtle – not like Disneyland', Meyer assures us.

The rest of the hotel, however, seems to reject this burst of technology in the lobby. Occupying an adjacent area is a traditional library where guests find not only novels but also issues of *National Geographic* and academic literature, which Meyer and Van Vliet consider an important aspect of the hotel's focus on wellbeing. Next to the library are meeting rooms that also hark back to tradition; the design of these spaces is based on personal contact and inspired by Parisian salons. A highlight of the food and

beverage area is a market that carries locally sourced produce. 'Just a decade ago, eating food from the other side of the planet was seen as a luxury. In the future it will be a luxury to eat healthy, organic food from around the corner of your hotel,' says Meyer. It's all about a sense of place and time, and engaging the five senses reinforces this idea. Instead of a wine bar, CO has a tearoom – inspired by the ancient Asian *chaikhana* – where you can match the flavour of your tea to the pastry or sandwich you choose. From this point, guests make their way through the open kitchen and enter the courtyard, which is surrounded by rest rooms that provide private views of the garden.

The duo is also looking at different ways to save money that will have a positive impact on guests. 'Most travellers say the most important

thing during their hotel stay is a good night's sleep,' says Meyer. 'But when developers work out the costs of a hotel and see that x number of rooms multiplied by x number of beds adds up to a lot of money, they often go for a cheaper alternative to save some cash. We would rather give people a beautiful night's sleep and remove the things they're less likely to want or need, such as a minibar stocked with items costing three times their value.' A comfortable bed is, therefore, the most important feature in the bedroom, along with a lighting scheme that mimics a natural sunrise and an audio track of birdsong.

It all sounds very Zen, but what about the deluge of water you use when relaxing in one of the baths in the suites? Meyer replies that 'people shouldn't be interrupted while bathing and >>>

IN THE HOTEL'S MULTIFUNCTIONAL DINING SPACES, SMALL GROUPS HAVE A CHOICE OF TABLE ARRANGEMENTS, WHILE COUPLES CAN OPT FOR THE PRIVACY OF A BOOTH.

THE BACK-TO-BASICS RETREAT FEATURES AN OPEN COURTYARD AT ITS CENTRE.

IN THE OPEN KITCHEN, CO'S CHEFS CREATE CUISINE FROM LOCAL PRODUCE.

'In the future luxury will be synonymous with time and health – neither of which can be bought'
Hans Meyer

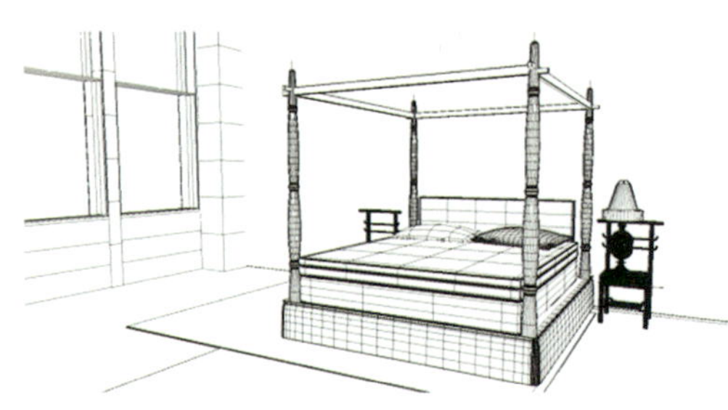

WIREFRAME RENDERINGS SHOW THE SPATIAL LAYOUT OF A BEDROOM.

THE BEDROOMS – ARGUABLY THE MOST IMPORTANT FEATURE OF ANY HOTEL – FEATURE EDWARD VAN VLIET'S ALKISTIS BED, ORIGINALLY DESIGNED FOR COCO-MAT.

reminded not to use too much water. They should still have a free choice. The responsibility is on us to figure out alternatives to the problem. Bath water from the suites could be reused for flushing toilets.'

Meyer and Van Vliet believe that although you can't prevent people from travelling, it's important to make today's destinations as sustainable as possible. And, while doing so, they want to create locally infused environments conducive to a healthy lifestyle. Each CO hotel is to have a character that is tied to the location, which the pair plans to convey by using a regional style when renovating existing buildings. The hotels will be fundamentally the same but locally different, and CO will utilize what is available close to a specific site. If the first hotel is in Amsterdam, for instance, where

an abundance of local produce and plants is available, the two men recognize a good opportunity to bring nature into the city in the form of a roof garden or greenhouse. 'The hotels should feel distinctively local,' says Meyer. 'If I'm in a city I want to feel like I'm there – and not anywhere else in the world.' ■

sevv.com
hotelsahead.com

THE SMALL COUCH, CALLED DIONI, WAS DESIGNED BY EDWARD VAN VLIET FOR COCO-MAT.

Wilkhahn

Automotive progress meets chair design. Chassis for work and life. wilkhahn.com/chassis

Perfection on
Legs

Chassis.
Design: Stefan Diez

CASCADE COIL DRAPERY

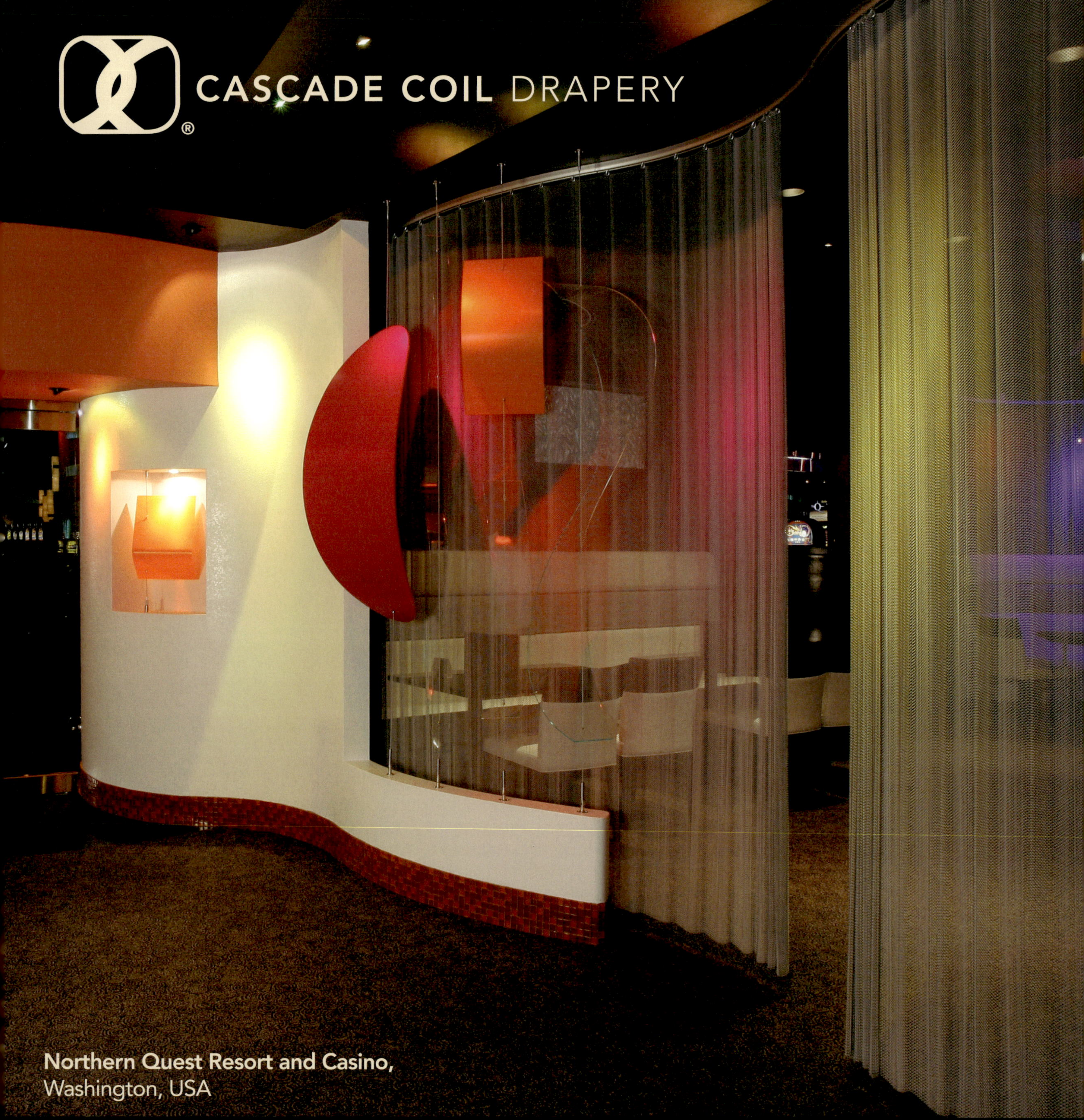

Woven wire fabric from Cascade Coil

Projects include multi-story wire mesh draperies for hotels, auditoriums, and casinos; curved dividers for visual merchandising; window treatments for private homes; safety & blast mitigation screening; sculptural forms for urban gardens; decorative interior/exterior wall coverings; solar shading for buildings and parking garages; aviary screening for animal habitats, and see-through appealing barriers for commercial security. Whatever the application, let us help you realize your creative vision.

www.cascadecoil.com | T +1.971.224.2188

No limits

Bolidtop® flooring:
unlimited interior design
The purpose or interior of public facility
buildings often changes throughout the
years. Appearances run from look to look.
Architecture is one discipline that makes
this happen, interior design another. Bolidt is the creator of sensational, aestheti-
cal and flexible Bolidtop® flooring systems
that easily enable magnificent re-use.
Liberating freedom to turn any creative
design idea into reality. Whether it is an
exhibition centre in Japan, an eatery in the
USA or a hotel lobby in Shanghai. Bolidt,
No limits.

www.bolidt.com

bolidt

Sospesi nel tempo
MASIERO
www.masierogroup.com
argine

morning dew

Design Kati Meyer-Brühl

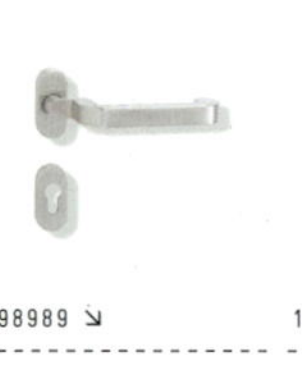

WWW.ARCHITONIC.COM

www.architonic.com/PRODUCT CODE

"THE BEST FRIEND ON EARTH OF MAN IS THE TREE.
WHEN WE USE THE TREE RESPECTFULLY AND ECONOMICALLY,
WE HAVE ONE OF THE GREATEST RESOURCES ON THE EARTH."
- Frank Lloyd Wright

Antique Oak Smoked - Suitable for underfloor heating

ebonyandco
handcrafted solid wood floors

www.ebonyandco.com

Amsterdam Herengracht 516 1017CC +31 (0)20 616 3444 amsterdam@ebonyandco.com
Worldwide Showrooms New York Dublin London Amsterdam Moscow Barcelona

STILLS

PORTFOLIO OF PLACES

WATCH HOW RYUJI NAKAMURA'S CORNFIELD INSTALLATION
TAKES SHAPE ON PAGE 082.
PHOTO COURTESY OF RYUJI NAKAMURA

THE LATEST MONKI CONCEPT IS AN UNDERWATER WORLD THAT
PROVIDES ROOM FOR THE BRAND'S COLLECTION OF PRODUCTS
AND ACCESSORIES.

MONKI 3
SEA OF SCALLOPS

BY ELECTRIC DREAMS

The theme that design agency Electric Dreams conjured up for the interiors of the first Monki shops in 2006 was Peacock Fields (see *Frame* 61, page 158). Two years later, at a point when H&M had acquired 60 per cent of the Swedish brand, Monki's retail environment reflected a new scenario: the City of Oil and Steel (see *Frame* 64, page 132). A significant expansion of the label's line of products and accessories demanded a third concept and, consequently, an interior separated into four areas. According to Catharina Frankander of Electric Dreams, visitors to Monki now find an underwater world where 'dangerous currents, sparkling jellyfish, glowing bubbles and sunken merry-go-rounds mark the shoe, accessory, jeans and campaign departments. A major challenge was the visual merchandiser's desire to rotate the store's garments every day and to work with different themed campaigns throughout the year.' The solution includes wheeled 'display horses', which are easy to move through the Sea of Scallops, and 'shimmery lilies' above all the tables: props and graphics hung from these flowers can be changed as often as needed.

electricdreams.se

WORDS **FEMKE DE WILD**
PHOTOS **FREDRIK SWEGER**

bricks
the modular system

a new workspace philosophy

THE LOCAL FIRM'S POP-UP STORE IN STOCKHOLM BUILDS ON THE FASHION BRAND'S INVESTIGATIONS INTO DEMATERIALIZATION.

AS THE PLOT UNFOLDS

BY 42 AND THE LOCAL FIRM

United by their Swedish roots, The Local Firm, an up-and-coming fashion label, and London-based architecture collective 42 designed an installation to mark the final weeks of the clothing brand's pop-up store in Stockholm. Architect Johan Berglund says that 42's affinity for The Local Firm's aesthetic – the Cold War meets Bauhaus – prompted a graphic composition comprising a series of rectangles. Entitled 'As the Plot Unfolds', the installation imagines a room in the making, using notional wall elements made from open frames as the only spatial dividers. The creation of the room has been paused in a pre-clad state, and the rectangles form layered, framed views of the shop interior. Visitors open up these frames to 'unfold' the room. 'Both architecture and fashion are concerned with different types of cladding and façades,' says Berglund. 'Both disciplines work with wrapping and enclosing "bodies", and the collaboration is most successful when architecture functions as a backdrop, conceptually reinforcing the clothing rather than overpowering it.'

42architects.com

WORDS **TRACEY INGRAM**
PHOTOS **COURTESY OF 42 ARCHITECTS**

PHOTO ALEXANDER DAHL

THE MANOLOS ARE DISPLAYED ATOP SHINING PEDESTALS AND SUSPENDED ON GOLDEN RODS.

MANOLO BLAHNIK

BY DATA NATURE

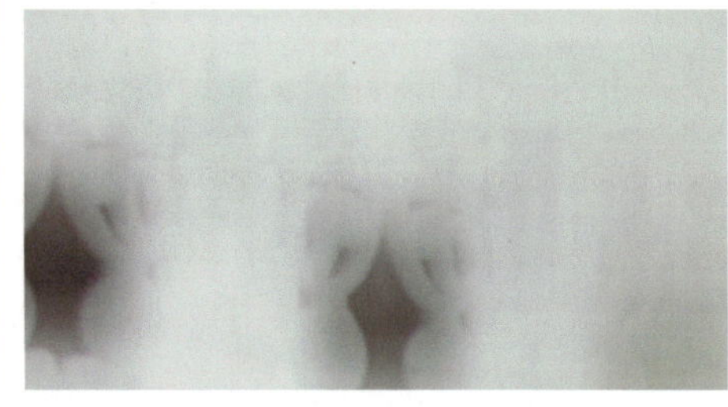

'In our latest project for fashion icon Manolo Blahnik, we used the idea of a dacha, which is quite rough and simple in a way, and contrasted it with something very delicate,' says Nick Leith-Smith, cofounder of Data Nature. The brief for the 73-m^2 store in Moscow's Tretiakov Plaza asked for an environment that the shoes could 'inhabit', yet a place with a sense of provenance. 'Manolo is against spatial cloning,' explains Leith-Smith. Glazed on three sides, the shop is effectively a box within a box. The timber used on the frontage represents the traditional dacha, while the CNC-milled Corian panels inside are emblematic of Russian lace. 'We needed a material that was translucent and would work even at this level of detail,' he continues. Amid all the ornament, however, customers aren't allowed to forget what they've come for: backed by wooden screens, the all-important footwear takes pride of place.

datanature.com

WORDS **GRANT GIBSON**
PHOTOS **COURTESY OF DATA NATURE**

LE

LIMITED EDITION
Living floors

CARPET FLASH GREY MATERIAL 100% COWHIDE MADE IN BELGIUM

WWW.LE.BE

STELLA MCCARTNEY

BY GILES MILLER

Giles Miller is a young designer who has become synonymous with a very specific material: cardboard. 'It's something I've grown to love more and more because of the extent to which I've used it,' he confesses. 'The corrugation is really what interests me, because it's a very cleverly engineered material that's also cheap and readily available. Everybody knows it so well that it's kind of overlooked.' Miller puts the material to good use, though. His latest project is a pop-up installation for a Stella McCartney shop-in-shop at the Galleries Lafayette on Boulevard Haussmann in Paris. Miller opted for two cardboard elements: bold lettering between 1.5 and 2 m tall in a variety of fonts, and ten cubes featuring gold-leafed faces and surfaces finished in a hatch corrugated pattern the designer describes as 'fluted'. Initially meant as a temporary installation for Paris, the assemblage has since travelled to Selfridges in London and is bound for Asia as well. 'It's doing more of a tour than was originally intended,' says a modest Miller, 'which is quite nice.'

gilesmiller.com

WORDS **GRANT GIBSON**
PHOTOS **RICHARD CORCORAN**

Today I open with Arc*.

Beta
design Joe Colombo

Living
design Dominique Perrault
Gaelle Lauriot Prevost

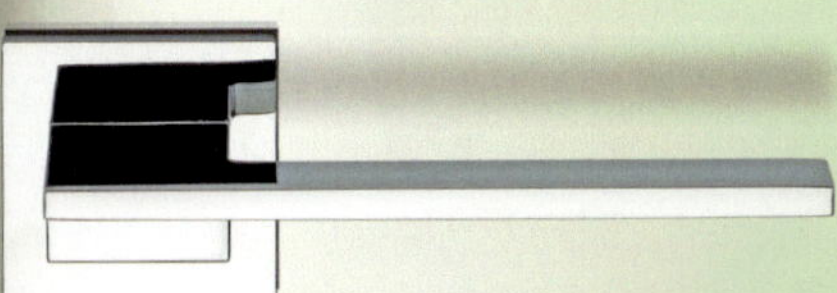

✱ **Arc**
design Rodolfo Dordoni

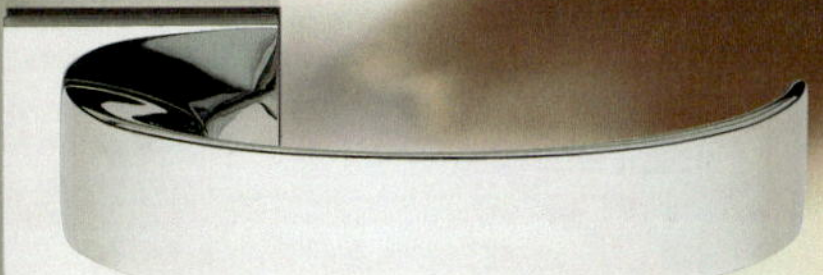

Planet
design Luca Casini

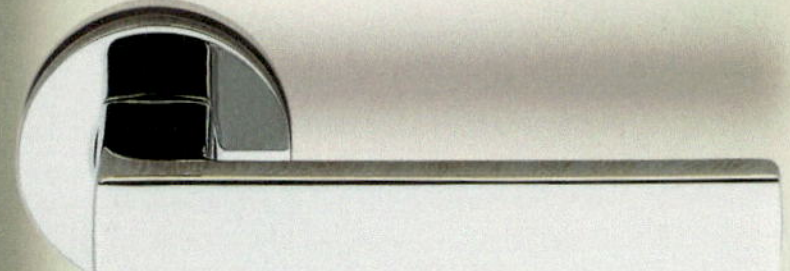

HANS BOODT.
CREATING CHARACTERS

THE GOODS SPACE HOUSES AN EVER-CHANGING
SELECTION OF ITEMS - HENCE THE NEUTRAL BACKGROUND.

GOODS

BY ANTONIO GARDONI

A grey wall wraps a store interior in an outlet village near Brescia. Set 60 cm into the space, the wall forms a second skin. Installed behind it is a wealth of display elements. 'Grey was necessary because various brands will occupy the store in turn,' says architect Antonio Gardoni, who renovated the space, called Goods. 'The products showcased could be sportswear one month and crockery the next, so the background had to be neutral.' Grey is also somewhat provocative, as it is the polar opposite of the on-trend colours being used by neighbouring retailers in the centre. 'Other shops scream for attention. Goods doesn't, but the grey makes it stand out nonetheless,' says Gardoni. Adding a lightning bolt of colour is a yellow coating applied to all niches and display elements, whether pullout shelving, drawers or clothing rails. Even when parts of the display system are not in use, glimpses of yellow create a sense of expectation. 'It's "supermarket yellow",' says Gardoni, 'It'll probably clash with some products, but it goes with the DIY aesthetic of this roller-painted, plastic-laminated ply interior.'

antoniogardoni.com

WORDS **CHARLOTTE VAUDREY**
PHOTOS **OTTAVIO TOMASINI**

PROPERTY OF...

BY RICHARD CHAMBERLAIN AND PETER TEO

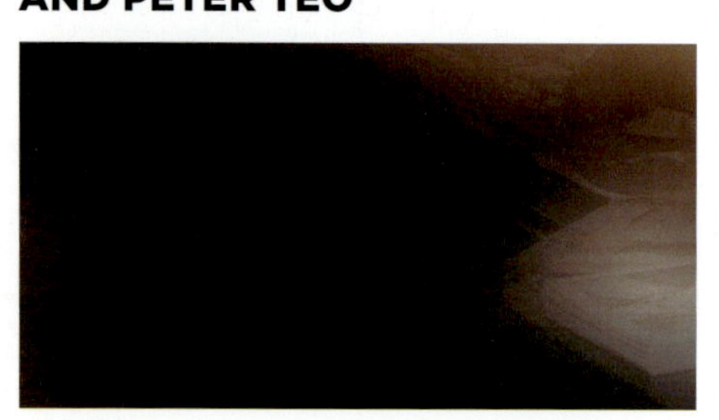

It seems as if less is *not* more for designers Richard Chamberlain and Peter Teo. The Singapore-based duo, who have a clothing range and a small string of cafés, branched out even further in 2006 with the launch of their collection of men's bags and accessories, which bear the 'Property Of' brand name. Noticing a distinct lack of bag options in the male market, Chamberlain and Teo visualized what they themselves would want to use. While the pair may stamp their signature style on everything, these products appear distinctly unbranded. A subtly embossed brand name is often all that graces the goods, hinting at the user to make his own mark – if he can bring himself, that is, to etch into a handsome expanse of expensive leather.

A sense of ownership is what drives the brand. Intrigued by the unique characters passing through their three signature coffee shops, the partners devised an image that focuses on the identity of the product owner, rather than that of the designer. Their advertising campaigns match this mantra, and in a recent example bags and their contents were photographed alongside their owners. The concept captured the company's obsession with the individual.

This year Chamberlain and Teo opened a new store in Amsterdam after being captivated by an empty corner shop in an up-and-coming neighbourhood near the retail-rich Nine Streets area. 'We wanted to put people at ease by incorporating a blend of design elements that are visually and emotionally familiar,' says Chamberlain. 'Not all our stores will look the same, but we do want them to *feel* the same.' Just as the bags fuse old and new design values, the European flagship store in Amsterdam combines old and new materials, while reflecting its café-cum-store origins. Walking into the shop, which is dominated by a serving counter, you'd be hard pressed to identify what's original and what's not. Is it an old restaurant that's been left mostly intact, with new stock artistically placed throughout the interior? Was the space previously something else? Are the serving-style elements additions?

A certain ambiguity is intentional. The space was, in fact, essentially a bare room before Chamberlain and Teo took over and converted it into a new home for their beloved bags. The new (yet old-looking) classic counter is offset by vintage tiles, reused lampshades and antique cabinetry. The project was a compromise between the genuine antiques they managed to source and the newer items that had to be 're-created' and aged. Mirrors appear to have succumbed to the relentless march of time when they are actually brand new. Like a forgotten menu, a series of names inscribed on the mirrors includes individuals who worked on the project – more of that personal touch. Every corner of the shop has been well considered, right down to the classic toilet. These designers are sticklers for consistency.

The store is an extension of the company's delight in all that is understated. The absence of shelving gives the appearance of products displayed in an accidental way. Leather goods sit casually atop restaurant chairs, on the serving counter and along window ledges. 'It's meant to look as if someone could have just left his bag behind after grabbing a coffee,' says Hendrik Stroscher, the brand's Amsterdam agent and project manager.

The café in Chamberlain and Teo's Singapore shop has generated a considerable amount of 'extra' income. At present, the Amsterdam flagship's facilities don't allow for a fully functioning dining experience, but you can get a damn good cup of renowned Stumptown coffee while you browse. With this combination of elements, 'we can attract new customers who otherwise might not be considered our typical target market,' says Chamberlain. 'We've noticed no confusion, and visitors seem happy to hang out in the space as they would in a café. Every project tends to reinforce our view that real discovery is the ability to see the same horizon with new eyes.'

thepropertyof.com

WORDS **TRACEY INGRAM**
PHOTO **JORIS BRURING**

"THE BEST FRIEND ON EARTH OF MAN IS THE TREE.
WHEN WE USE THE TREE RESPECTFULLY AND ECONOMICALLY,
WE HAVE ONE OF THE GREATEST RESOURCES ON THE EARTH."

- Frank Lloyd Wright

Walnut Country Ultramatt · Suitable for underfloor heating

ebonyandco
handcrafted solid wood floors

www.ebonyandco.com

Amsterdam Herengracht 516 1017CC +31 (0)20 616 3444 amsterdam@ebonyandco.com
Worldwide Showrooms New York Dublin London Amsterdam Moscow Barcelona

JSPR

STEEL CABINETS

WWW.JSPR.EU

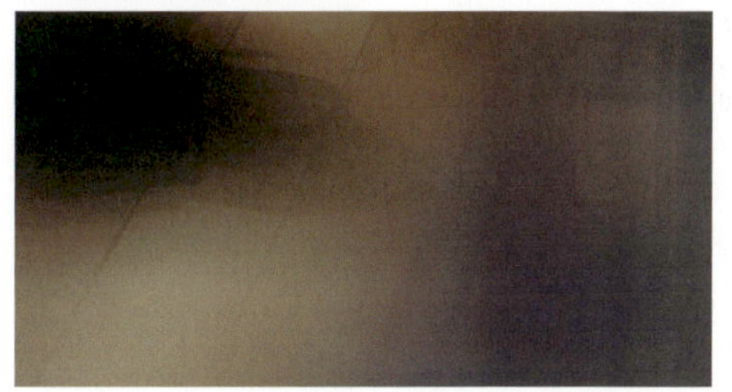

AN OLD CHURCH PEW AS FRONT DESK, A CHANDELIER CASCADE OF VINTAGE LAMPSHADES, A LADDER REVEALING ITS ORIGINS: THIS IS HOSTEM.

HOSTEM

BY JAMESPLUMB

'Our hearts sank when we first entered the space,' recalls Hannah Plumb, one half of artist-designer duo JamesPlumb. She's referring to the East End premises that she and James Russell recently transformed into a boutique. 'There was not one original feature left or waiting to be discovered.' No. 43 Redchurch Street, London, had been a Bengali family's living room, a storage facility, an insurance broker's office and an art gallery, to name but a few of its incarnations. Currently, as independent menswear store Hostem, its three storeys have a well-worn, eclectic yet discreetly luxurious look: think reclaimed-timber floorboards, walls and ceiling draped in aged canvas panels, bare metal rails and caged light bulbs. Other delightful flourishes include old railway-conductor bags filled with white concrete, now serving as plinths, and a pair of steel barrel trolleys salvaged from a brewery to provide seating. It may have been their first commercial project, but Plumb and Russell have carried it off with aplomb, whimsy and personality.

jamesplumb.co.uk

WORDS **GIOVANNA DUNMALL**
PHOTOS **ANDREW MEREDITH**

CUBIC

GRAPHICS PROVIDE VISUAL INTEREST IN H&M OSAKA'S 'DEAD' AREAS AND WAITING ZONES.

H&M

BY A-B-D AND SARA HILDÉN BENGTSSON

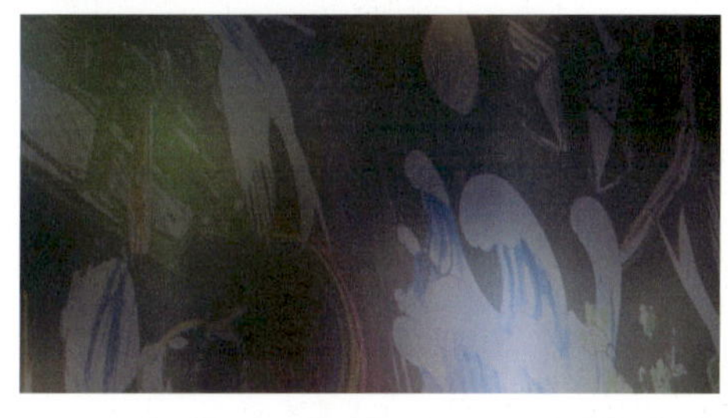

H&M's Osaka store is more about the graphics on the walls than the walls themselves. A-B-D's Fredrik Bengtsson explains why.

What is the spatial experience like for visitors?
The illustrations [by Lovisa Burfitt] help to guide people through the store in an unusual way. Each wall features a tailor-made scribble suitable for the area. We placed graphics where customers have time to read the words: waiting for the lift or standing in line at the cash desk.

Graphics are the main focus of the space. What does this say about fashion retailers?
In my opinion, there is a risk that large retail brands can become static when entering a new market or country. In the case of a big retail chain, adding graphics to the store injects more personality and excitement into the space, while also describing what type of customer the brand wants to attract.

What do you think lies ahead for interior graphics?
Graphics and navigation are synonymous. The two should act as a strong unit rather than as a layer you add afterwards. From a branding perspective, store graphics are set to play a huge role in retail chains. It's a lot easier to change walls than furniture. The rapid changes in regard to 'what's in' and 'what's out' make graphics more convenient. Environmental branding and retail aren't just about logos and brand colours. A combination of materials, shapes and surfaces is necessary to communicate the brand.

a-b-d.se

WORDS **TRACEY INGRAM**
PHOTOS **COURTESY OF A-B-D**

A KINETIC, MIRRORED CEILING DESIGNED BY RANDOM INTERNATIONAL IN COLLABORATION WITH RENE GONZALEZ DEFINES ALCHEMIST'S AIRY BUT URBAN INTERIOR.

ALCHEMIST

BY RENE GONZALEZ

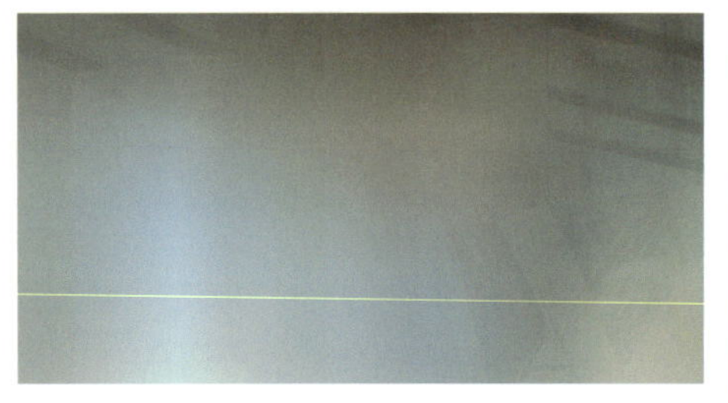

Miami is not known for understatement, so Herzog & de Meuron's new, mixed-use concrete parking garage, airy and threaded with light, comes as a surprise. It looks naked in an un-made-up and un-worked-out way – effortless. Similarly, set into the building's fifth floor is Alchemist, a simple glass box designed by local architect Rene Gonzalez. It too is radically exposed: the concept boutique's predominantly mirror-clad surfaces reflect the street below and the city's tropi-corporate skyline, a canvas the consistency of mercury against which clothes on display materialize as the only solid, static objects in space. Shards of pedestrians and automobiles, high-rises and clouds are thrown into motion through a kinetic mirror installation. Sensors set 43 mirrored pneumatic panels rippling overhead in sync with browsing customers, pausing when they pause, mimicking their movements. 'You feel like you're caught up in the movement of the cars on the garage ramps, the hustle and bustle of the street below,' says Gonzalez, 'and – simultaneously – floating in the sky.'

renegonzalezarchitect.com

WORDS **SHONQUIS MORENO**
PHOTOS **MICHAEL STAVARIDIS**

Light Changer+

ERCO's DALI technology makes lighting control energy-efficient, user-friendly and economical: efficient visual comfort through intelligent light management. Timer programs, sensor technology and light scenes tailored to suit specific situations unlock enormous potential for energy saving. The new Light Changer+ with its large colour touchscreen makes operating the ERCO Light System DALI even simpler and more convenient to use than ever before. The graphic user interface sets the benchmark for design and functionality. Powerful lighting control systems that the user intuitively understands and effectively uses is where the future of digitally controlled architectural lighting is to be found.

www.erco.com

20 Years

BRANDVAN
® EGMOND

BRAND VAN EGMOND
Nikkelstr. 41, 1411 AH Naarden NL
T +31 (0)35 692 12 59
F +31 (0)35 691 17 25
info@brandvanegmond.com

Digital Dreams

ENTERING GARETH PUGH'S FIRST STORE IS LIKE 'WALKING INTO A GIANT TELEVISION SCREEN', SAYS IWAN HALSTEAD OF DAYTRIP.

GARETH PUGH

BY **DAYTRIP**

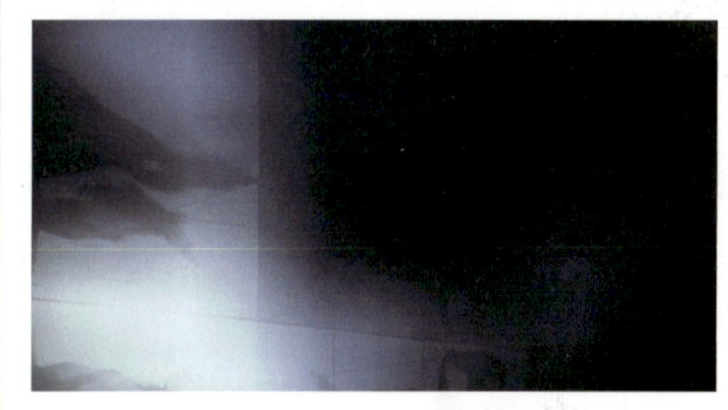

Daytrip adopted the colour of night for the design of Gareth Pugh's debut store in Hong Kong. Pugh's creations are showcased in a black, mirrored cube that is dominated by a floor-to-ceiling LED wall. Reels of the designer's collaborations with video artist Ruth Hogben continually stream throughout the space, bouncing infinite reflections onto walls, ceiling and floor. Much like Pugh's fashions, texture and contrast guide the retail design: juxtapositions in the interior see dark meet light and matte greet glossy. Visitors passing through the dimly lit main space find stark clinical lighting in the fitting rooms, where padded triangular tiles in ash-grey leather are visually multiplied by angled mirrors. The result is a rather contorted asylum for trying on fashions by Pugh. A façade of matte-black rubber encases a large glass window that promotes the brand against a constantly changing video backdrop.

daytripstudio.com

WORDS **TRACEY INGRAM**
PHOTOS **JOSEPH CHEUNG**

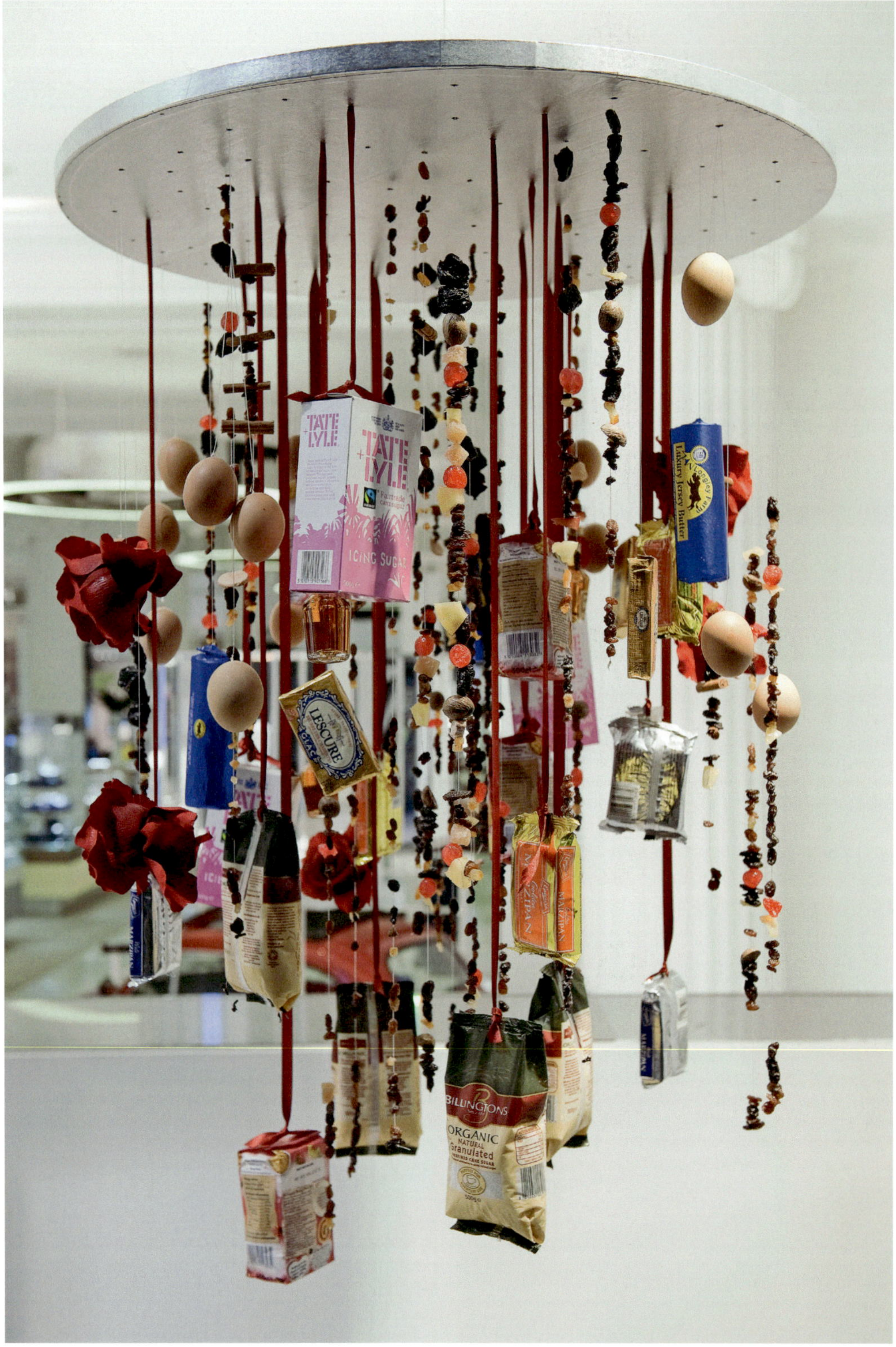

SELFRIDGES

BY KYLE BEAN

In one of his most ambitious projects to date, Brighton-based designer Kyle Bean installed a number of sculptural scenes in the windows of department store Selfridges in Oxford Street, London. The five distinctive displays were inspired by the theory that 'matter cannot be created or destroyed, only transformed'. Expressing the idea of what he calls 'the law of conservation of mass' in the shop windows, Bean juxtaposed alternate incarnations of the same materials, hanging them side by side on a pair of scales to illustrate their equal weight. One of the works included a wedding cake hanging next to a mobile made of its ingredients, while another showed suspended fairy-tale books balanced with a fantasy castle made from their pages. With the castle, as with the chair crafted from a cardboard box, Bean used his trademark

paper-crafting skills. The most intricate and visually arresting work, however, occupying pride of place in the corner window, was a Honda Fireblade motorcycle suspended next to all of its individual components. 'I wanted passers-by to get the picture instantly,' says Bean, who was commissioned by Selfridges after pitching the department store an idea. 'And hopefully, people will find an element of humour in it, too.'

kylebean.co.uk

WORDS **CASSANDRA PIZZEY**
PHOTOS **ANDREW MEREDITH**

A HONDA FIREBLADE HANGS IN SELLFRIDGES' CORNER WINDOW IN ITS RECOGNIZABLE STATE NEXT TO A MOBILE MADE FROM ALL ITS COMPONENTS.

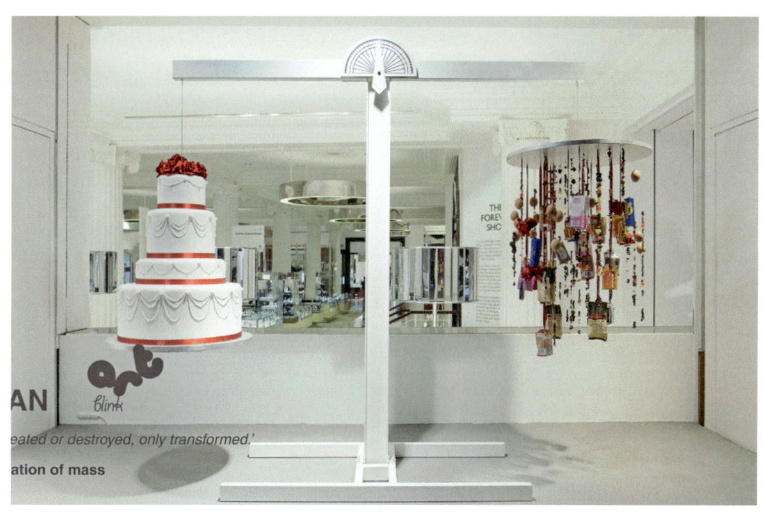

Quartz planks

Mosa. Tiles.

HARVEY NICHOLS

BY HARVEY NICHOLS DESIGN TEAM

Inspired by autumn/winter catwalk shows by the likes of Stella McCartney and Céline, Harvey Nichols recently featured some 'understated classics' in its window displays in its store in Knightsbridge, London. 'We have turned the current "classics" trend on its head to transform mundane objects into works of art,' says Janet Wardley, head of visual display at the fashionable department store. Everyday items cobbled together to create larger-than-life objects included a huge hammer covered in nails, a tree made of pencils and a piano crafted from cassette tapes. Spicing up the scenes were giant-size models of nails, pencils, tapes and so forth, further emphasizing the theme of 'Everyday Design'. At first glance, the bright-orange Ferrari seemed to have backed straight into the shop window, but a closer look revealed a car made from thousands of tiny plastic horses. This and other splashes of orange provided the only colour in the windows which where kept neutral, letting the fashions speak for themselves.

harveynichols.com

WORDS **CASSANDRA PIZZEY**
PHOTOS **MICHAEL TAYLOR**

VILLA KANOUSAN

BY YUUSUKE KARASAWA

'Houses represent architectural philosophy in the most concise way,' says architect Yuusuke Karasawa. 'Here I used an algorithmic method based on a spatial model applicable to products and buildings alike.' The weekend house on a hill in Kimitsu, Japan, has four rooms on the ground floor and four upstairs. Four cubes are stacked in two layers, and additional cubes – inserted into wall-ceiling-floor intersections – penetrate the space, resulting in a seamless whole. The angles of the cubes are controlled by an algorithm that creates diversity and order within the interior. The algorithm is determined by the slope of the site, including the undulations in its surface, which are reflected in the angle of each cube. Occupants feel surrounded by – and part of – the outdoor environment.

yuusukekarasawa.com

WORDS MASAAKI TAKAHASHI
PHOTOS SERGIO PIRRONE

associated.nl

BY **JSPR**

THE STAIRCASE EXTENDS TO WALLS AND CEILING, INCREASING THE SENSE OF SPACIOUSNESS WITHIN THE RELATIVELY SMALL NEW KYOTO TOWN HOUSE.

NEW KYOTO TOWN HOUSE

BY ALPHAVILLE

Built on a long site with a narrow frontage in central Kyoto, Japan, where landscape-preservation rules are strict, New Kyoto Town House by Alphaville has an inconspicuous façade, which conceals an avant-garde interior design. Rooms occupying the building's three levels seem to have been shifted horizontally and vertically before being stacked. Partition walls are three-dimensional and slanted, accentuating the segmented residential environment and generating a sense of spaciousness. The staircase consists of polyhedrons featuring triangular components made of light-gauge steel. Extending to the floor, wall and ceiling, the staircase reflects light from the north and south into the centre of the building. 'My aim was to create volume in this high-density space, not to design decoration,' says Kentaro Takeguchi of Alphaville. Like a playground, the interior of this house provides occupants with things to duck under or trace with the hand while moving from one area to another.

a-ville.net

WORDS **MASAAKI TAKAHASHI**
PHOTOS **SERGIO PIRRONE**

STRAIT STREET CONVENIENCE

BY **CHRIS BRIFFA**

A public loo doesn't seem the most likely place for an art exhibition, but that's just what you'll find in the heart of Valletta, Malta. 'We noticed the deplorable state of municipal facilities on the island,' says architect Chris Briffa, 'and decided to turn this public convenience into a cultural convenience.' The small building provides room for two exhibition spaces: a stage to the back of the entrance area and a window display facing the street. Adorning the entrance hall, an installation by Norbert Attard blares the words 'I Love Tracy Emin' in large neon letters that can be read back to front or vice versa. Windows feature Attard's *V*, a work based on the eponymous novel by Thomas Pynchon. The Strait Street loo is the first of five similar projects on the island 'If all the toilets run art shows at the same time, we'll have a network of cultural attractions,' says a hopeful Briffa.

chrisbriffa.com

WORDS **CASSANDRA PIZZEY**
PHOTOS **COURTESY OF CHRIS BRIFFA AND NORBERT ATTARD**

NORBERT ATTARD'S ART INSTALLATIONS REFER TO THE TOILET'S LOCATION IN THE FORMER RED-LIGHT DISTRICT.

High tech so beautiful.
Elegance top performing.
This is Italy, when she wants to.

company:
Piavevetro srl
product line:
I AM
product name:
crystal sculptures
handcrafted in:
Italy
website:
iampiavevetro.com
contact:
info@iampiavevetro.com

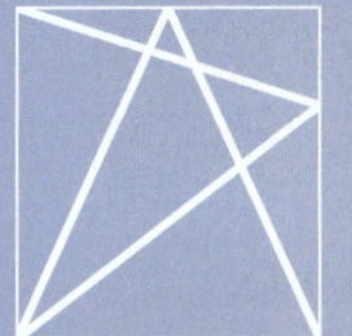

tilt and turn window

pivot-window

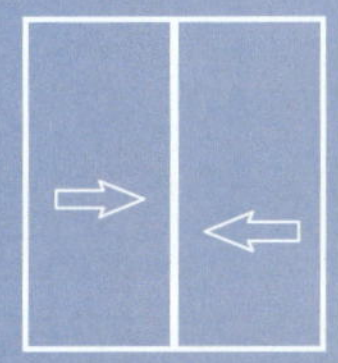

sliding-door

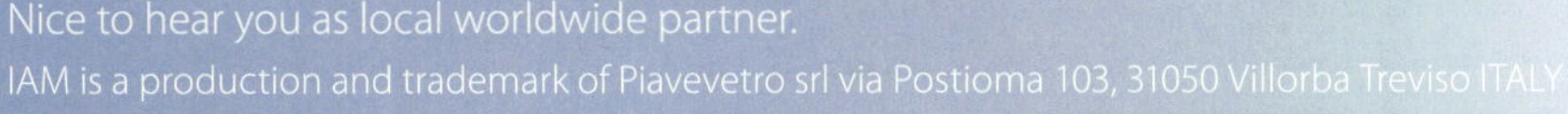

Nice to hear you as local worldwide partner.
IAM is a production and trademark of Piavevetro srl via Postioma 103, 31050 Villorba Treviso ITALY

HIGHLIGHTING CHEAP MONDAY'S NEW HEADQUARTERS IS A FELT-CLAD PYRAMID THAT IS USED AS A MEETING ROOM.

CHEAP MONDAY

BY UGLYCUTE

Although pyramids are anything but expressions of non-hierarchical organizations, it is this geometric shape that Uglycute chose as the main architectural feature of the new HQ they designed for Swedish denim brand Cheap Monday. The centrepiece of the firm's 600-m^2 premises in Stockholm is a 4-m-high pyramid clad in needlepunch felt. 'We thought it would be interesting to build something special. A pyramid, yes. But what should we do with it?' explains Jonas Nobel of Uglycute. Despite the lack of windows and tables, the pyramid has turned out to be an ideal meeting room. It doesn't function as a control room in the manner of the average transparent conference room marking the middle of an office landscape. 'Since you can't see that anyone is actually having a meeting inside, the pyramid is also a sign of trust,' says Nobel, grinning. 'In other words, enter at your own risk.'

uglycute.com

WORDS **DANIEL GOLLING**
PHOTOS **MIKAEL OLSSON**

OBJECT CARPET | Rechbergstrasse 19 | D-73770 Denkendorf | Fon +49 (0) 711/34 02-0 | Fax +49 (0) 711/34 02-155 | www.object-carpet.com
NEW WEB ART PEBBLE BEACH 500
available in 7 colours
OBJECT CARPET

FIVE TRANSPARENT, PREFAB GREENHOUSES FUNCTIONED AS SMALL, FREESTANDING GALLERIES AT THE KOGEI TRIENNIAL.

KOGEI TRIENNIAL

BY NENDO

Can traditional Japanese crafts compete with modern Japanese design? The first International *Kogei* Triennial, an exhibition held earlier this year at the Museum of Contemporary Art in Kanazawa, did its best to champion the cause of crafts. The organizers asked young Oki Sato of Nendo to design the venue. Sato deliberately chose not to employ old-fashioned methods to create a showcase for traditional products. By placing five large, plastic, freestanding greenhouses in the exhibition space, he provided each of the five curators with a flexible, easy-to-arrange gallery. 'The *kogei* pieces are handmade, whereas these prefabricated greenhouses are mass-produced,' says Oki Sato, emphasizing the contrast between the items on display and his exhibition design. The objects inside the five structures were subtly illuminated, and the greenhouses themselves beckoned visitors like glowing lanterns. Black-carpeted aisles threaded their way among the greenhouses, partitioning the space into parcels of 'farmland'. This is 'a metaphor for the museum's hope that traditional crafts will continue to grow and flourish like plants', says Sato.

nendo.jp

WORDS **CATHELIJNE NUIJSINK**
PHOTOS **DAICI ANO**

RITRATTO DI FAMIGLIA IN UN INTERNO
SISTEMA ALL DAY / ALL NIGHT
md house
MD HOUSE Via Durante, 28 . Prata di Pordenone . PN . Italy . tel.+39 0434.620481 www.mdhouse.it
ALL design Hot-Des SAIL design Mario Mazzer Ph. Miro Zagnoli Ad. Art Work Studio

Link…
Architecture on the ceiling.
Design by Ramón Esteve

Just like the skyline of a big city, the four modules of Link
can be combined to create silhouettes and volumes
on the ceiling, fitting every space and situation.
It only requires a single power connection point and use dimmable,
efficient light sources.

Visit www.vibia.es, all information and 3D files are already available.

VIBIA

UNIVERSE OF PARTICLES

BY ATELIER BRÜCKNER

An interactive exhibition designed by Atelier Brückner is the latest attraction at CERN: the European Organization for Nuclear Research. Thousands of visitors make their way to the centre each year, curious about the Large Hadron Collider (LHC) housed 100 m below the ground. Comparing subatomic particles with the inconceivable vastness of the solar system, the displays attempt to shed light on the complex scientific experiments being conducted within the building. Universe of Particles transports visitors into a world without scale, from microcosm to macrocosm. Seemingly seamless spheres appear to float freely throughout the 450-m² space like the planets of a solar system, and the highlight of the exhibition is a multimedia show that invites visitors to experience the phenomenon of the Big Bang. 'We have entered the reactive-media period,' explains designer Professor Uwe Brückner. 'Instead of standard touchscreens, we developed globe-shaped showcases for this project, featuring curved, back-projected touch-sensitive surfaces to convey information.' It's 'information on demand', he says.

atelier-brueckner.de

WORDS **TRACEY INGRAM**
PHOTOS **MICHAEL JUNGBLUT**

A SERIES OF CORIAN AND ACRYLIC-RESIN SPHERES HOUSE ARTEFACTS AND FUNCTION AS INTERACTIVE ELEMENTS AT CERN'S UNIVERSE OF PARTICLES EXHIBITION.

PHOTO COURTESY OF RYUJI NAKAMURA

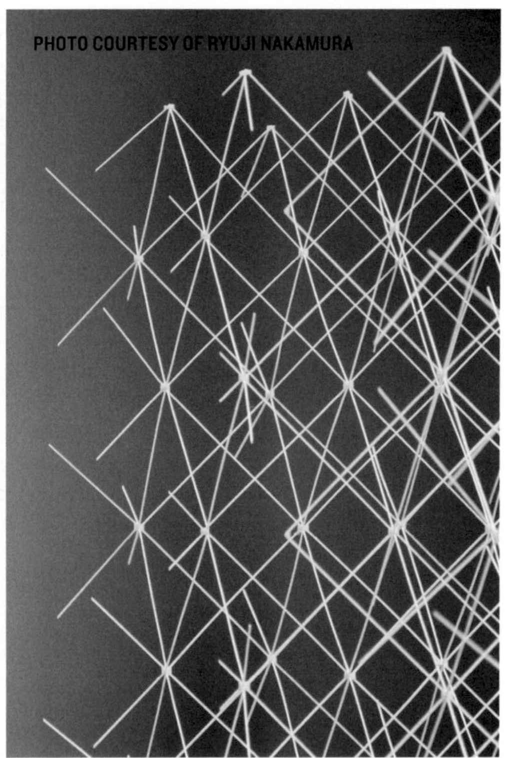

TRIANGULAR IN FORM, CORNFIELD FEATURES A PLAY OF LINES THAT GIVES IT A DIFFERENT APPEARANCE FROM EVERY POINT OF VIEW.

CORNFIELD

BY RYUJI NAKAMURA

Ryuji Nakamura's contribution to the Where is Architecture? exhibition at The National Museum of Modern Art, Tokyo, is an extremely delicate but impressive three-dimensional work of art that occupies a roomy 54 m^2. 'Cornfield is a self-supporting structure that acts as a filter between the existing pillars of the exhibition space,' says Nakamura. The realization process was, to put it mildly, sheer drudgery. It took 100 volunteers one month to glue together the 1.7-mm, laser-cut paper ribs. The result is a dazzling play of lines that reveals an installation with a completely different appearance from every point of view. The size transcends that of all earlier designs by Nakamura. 'I made light and thin structures before, but this one is massive,' says a delighted Nakamura. 'Although it's made of thousands of small parts, it looks like one big volume. I wouldn't call it an object. It's more like an atmosphere.'

ryujinakamura.com

WORDS **CATHELIJNE NUIJSINK**
PHOTOS **DAICI ANO**

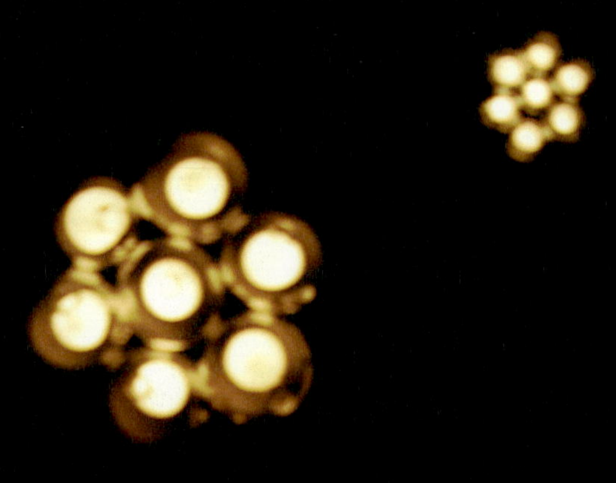

BOCCI IS AVAILABLE IN THE FINEST SHOPS ALL OVER EUROPE: VISIT WWW.BOCCI.CA

Antwerp	Edinburgh	Ingolstadt	Mainz	St. Gallen
Aubière	Effingham	Innsbruck	Manchester	Stockholm
Basel	Fiorano Modenese	Kloten	Milano	Stuttgart
Berlin	Frankfurt	Knokke	München	Torino
Bielefeld	Gent	Köln	Nürnberg	Tricesimo
Bilzen	Gistel	La Rochelle	Paris	Wageningen
Brussels	Graz	Limassol	Reggio Emilia	Wassenaar
Budapest	Hamburg	Linz	Salzburg	Wien (Vienna)
Copenhagen	Hamm	London	San Dona' di Piave	Winterthur
Dortmund	Harlingen	Lörrach	Simpelveld	Wolfsburg
Düsseldorf	Ibiza	Luzern	St. Etienne	Zürich

28 by Omer Arbel

+ 1.604.639.5185
www.bocci.ca
sales@bocci.ca

+ 49.151.2406.1212
www.bocci.ca
infoeu@bocci.ca

BOCCI Vancouver Berlin

Standard Fixtures and Custom Chandeliers
LED | Xenon | Halogen

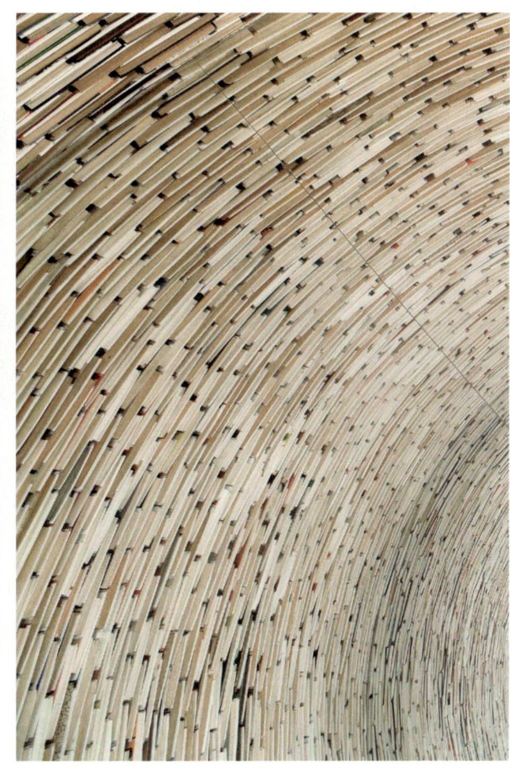

SCANNER

BY **MATEJ KRÉN**

Over 90,000 books stacked like bricks formed Matej Krén's *Scanner*, the Slovakian artist's tallest book sculpture to date. Standing more than 11 m tall, the monumental construction drastically altered the area it filled at Bologna's MAMbo (Museum of Modern Art). One by one, visitors edged their way through a narrow space, multiplied and obscured by a series of mirrors, that was created to cause a feeling of sensory vertigo. Krén plays with optical and perceptual illusions, often working on what he calls 'the boundary between physical and virtual space. A new situation emerges for the observer – a state of confusion between reality and fiction.' For Krén, books transmit knowledge and express the embodiment of our need to communicate with one another across space and time. In an age in which digital is taking over, the artist sees his work as 'an interface between the physical and virtual worlds'.

matejkren.cz

WORDS **TRACEY INGRAM**
PHOTOS **MATTEO MONTI**

MATEJ KRÉN USES MIRRORS TO MULTIPLY REFLECTIONS THAT EVOKE A 'FICTITIOUS EXTENSION OF REALITY'.

reincarnated

The 111 Navy Chair® with Coca-Cola™
Made from 111 recycled plastic bottles.
And 66 years of Emeco know-how.

 with 

emeco.net

Coca-Cola and the design of the Contour Bottle are trademarks of The Coca-Cola Company.

EXECUTED WITHIN FOUR DAYS, TAPE INSTALLATION #5 FEATURED 45 KM OF TRANSPARENT TAPE.

TAPE INSTALLATION #5

BY FOR USE/NUMEN

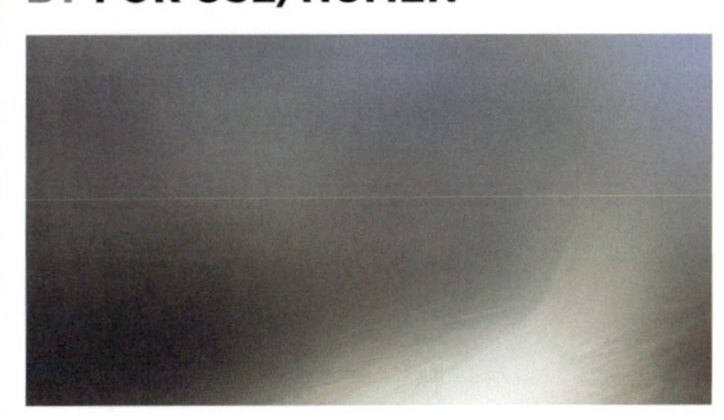

Designed by For Use/Numen, the tape installation series began as a set-design concept involving dancers who move among columns, stretching out lengths of tape that trace their trajectories to produce a (tape) recording of the choreography. For this year's DMY Design Festival in Berlin, the designers rolled out a new project, landing them first prize at the event. Multiple layers of tape formed a suspended cocoon strong enough for people to move through and explore.

A switch in venues forced a change of tactics, as the team's site-specific 'parasitic' installations usually cling to existing structures. In Berlin, the fifth maze of plastic tape was wrapped around scaffolding and, after construction, moved to its exhibition location via the old Tempelhof Airport runway. Despite the unforeseen restrictions, the team 'ended up having some fun with it', recalls designer Christoph Katzler. 'The sight of us pushing the installation down the runway evoked the image of a UFO landing at the airport.'

foruse.info

WORDS **TRACEY INGRAM**
PHOTOS **COURTESY OF FOR USE/NUMEN**

RECTANGLE, ELLIPSE & DISQUES

BY FELICE VARINI

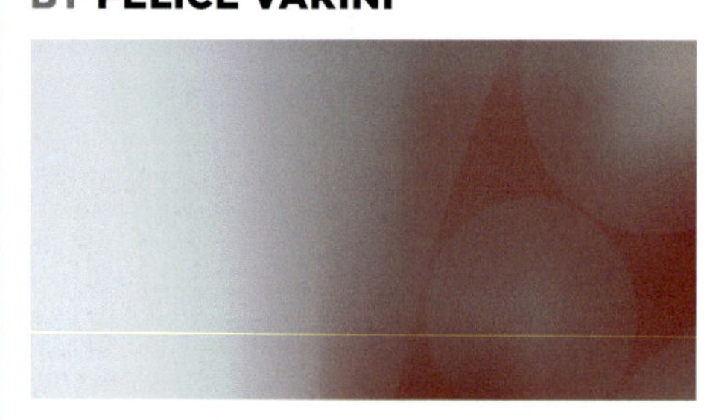

Felice Varini has vivified the staircase leading to Galerie Xippas in the Marais district of Paris with a striking red-and-white installation. The geometric form of *Rectangle, Ellipse & Disques* is coherent only at the bottom. As visitors climb the stairs to the first-floor gallery, the experience of viewing how the elements transform and extend over walls, ceilings and floorboards becomes an optical journey. 'What I like is to plunge the art lover into an intense, pictorial world as he or she traverses this narrow, intimate space in a solitary manner,' says the Swiss-born, Paris-based artist. 'The corridor becomes the canvas of a painting, playing with the reality that the architecture imposes.' Varini, now 58, has been adding abstract lines and shapes to architectural spaces since 1979. Another new installation is the 33.5-m-tall *Square with Four Circles*. Rising from Temple Plaza in New Haven, Connecticut, it is Varini's first outdoor public work in the USA.

varini.org

WORDS ANNA SANSOM
PHOTOS ANDRÉ MORIN

VARINI'S SERENE GEOMETRIC FORMS GIVE WAY TO INTENSE SWATHES OF COLOUR AS VISITORS ASCEND THE STAIRCASE.

Andrés Velencoso with
ORIGINAL SILESTONE®
KITCHEN WORKTOPS

SILESTONE®
by COSENTINO
THE ORIGINAL

SILESTONE
by COSENTINO
10 YEARS WARRANTY*

SILESTONE ADVANTAGES
HIGH RESISTANCE TO IMPACT
HIGH RESISTANCE TO ACIDS
HIGH RESISTANCE TO STAINING
MAXIMUM HYGIENE
NATURAL BEAUTY
WIDE RANGE OF COLOURS

QUARTZ WORKTOPS WITH ANTIBACTERIAL PROTECTION
COLOUR & DESIGN / DEMAND A GENUINE SILESTONE® WORKTOP
REJECT IMITATIONS / WITH THE COSENTINO GUARANTEE

WWW.SILESTONE.COM

* To activate the warranty service and to check terms and conditions please go to www.silestone.com

barcelona
world race

VISION
FASHION MANNEQUINS

ELITE COLLECTION

VitraHaus – welcome home.

There's a new source of design inspiration for every living space:
the VitraHaus. The new home to the Vitra Home Collection,
it features Vitra Classics and furnishings by contemporary designers.
VitraHaus, architects Herzog & de Meuron 2010

Frankfurt (3h)
Strasbourg (1h 30min)
Paris (3h 47min)
Vitra Campus
Freiburg (45min)
Munich (4h)
Basel (10min)
Zurich (1h)
Bern (1h)
Geneva (2h 25min)
Milan (3h 45min)

Visit the Vitra Campus in Weil am Rhein,
Germany (7 km from Basel). www.vitra.com/vitrahaus

vitra.

FEATURES

PROJECTS IN PERSPECTIVE

VISIT THE WATERHOUSE AT SOUTH BUND BY NHDRO ON PAGE 106.
PHOTO PEDRO PEGENAUTE

SECON

Old materials no longer die, but are increasingly incorporated into new structures.

WORDS **MATTHEW STEWART**

Sunlight streams through the warehouse skylight, falling softly on an interesting assortment of decorative iron grilles with flaked-off paint, crystal doorknobs, hinges and hooks, lamp fittings and other architectural bric-a-brac. Several salvaged doors rest against the wall, stripped of paint. Nearby, salvaged windows, stone flooring, plumbing, lighting and toilet bowls jostle for space. You'd be forgiven for mistaking this scene for the storeroom of an antique dealer or restoration specialist. In fact, though, the warehouse belongs to Brooklyn architects Made LLC, one of the most prominent young firms to emerge in New York City over the past decade.

Made's reputation rests on a series of residential projects that accommodate contemporary life within artfully restored, traditional town houses. Like increasing numbers of designers today, the architects at Made often opt for salvaged or reclaimed materials over new ones for their superior craftsmanship, authenticity and beauty in wear. Having developed a working environment and business model to facilitate their endeavours, they are a good example of the rapidly expanding and evolving landscape of material reuse, a growing field that is leading to a wholesale reconfiguration of the traditional method of sourcing and specifying architectural materials and finishes. Whereas 'recycled' used to denote a ramshackle hippy aesthetic, the new reuse is ready for the high end of design.

This development is being driven, of course, by the sustainable-design movement and the need to reduce the overall environmental impact of our design decisions. 'Using salvaged materials is the ultimate form of resource efficiency,' says Liz Ogbu, associate design director at Public Architecture. 'The environmental case is really clear. It is one of the few material options that satisfy the triple bottom line – environmental, economic and social – of sustainability.' Reclaimed materials not only save the energy otherwise required to produce new materials but also preserve the 'carbon sink' in the old materials. They are often less expensive to acquire. And there are social benefits as well: 'Working with locally sourced salvaged materials can help retain the cultural or social narrative of the community,' explains Ogbu. And, increasingly, it is being seen as an area ripe for so-called 'green collar' job growth.

Ogbu has become something of a leader

and spokesperson for this new movement. Her firm, Public Architecture, a non-profit-making organization based in San Francisco, has produced the *Design for Reuse Primer*. The project represents two years of research, funded in part by a grant from the U.S. Green Building Council. The volume, now available free of charge, is aimed at bridging the gap between the limited amount of highly technical information related to material reuse and consumer publications that may focus more on the appearance of these projects. 'Our aim was to help connect the dots,' says Ogbu.

These dots have emerged in all sectors of the building industry. They include a growing legion of contractors and building professionals advancing the practice of 'deconstruction', which, as an alternative to demolition, attempts the careful disassembly of buildings with the intent of preserving their materials for reuse. Deconstruction has boomed in recent years. The Building Material Reuse Association, which acts as a clearing house for information and resources related to the subject and sponsors the annual Decon conference, reports dramatic increases in attention from the architecture industry as well as from government agencies realizing the potential for new labour programmes related to deconstruction. Other dots include government agencies and subsidies or tax breaks attempting to bring a cost incentive to making use of old materials. Yet others involve material brokers such as Planet Reuse, services that have emerged to help connect designers and builders wishing to specify reused materials, and other sources of usable salvaged materials.

All this is not to say that all the barriers to material reuse have fallen completely. 'There is definitely more time involved,' says designer Matt Woods, whose interior for the Bloodwood restaurant (see page 096) made extensive use of salvaged materials for interior finishes. 'Unless you feel passionate about it, using reclaimed materials is going to be a more challenging way to go.' He's referring to the time involved not only in actually going out and finding materials to use, but also in customizing a design to fit materials whose dimensions may not be predictable at the outset of a project. While salvaged materials may often be less expensive than their new counterparts, or even free, this doesn't always translate directly into cost savings for the client. 'Don't forget, there's no such thing as a free lunch,' says Dave Hampton, a Chicago-based architect who regularly works with salvaged materials. 'If you're finding your own stuff, you may save on material costs, but in the long run you'll spend more time on planning. With custom pieces, somebody has to manage the process.'

Building codes have also served as a hindrance to a more widespread adoption of material reuse. Some building regulations simply prohibit the reuse of certain materials outright. Others may limit the types. Enterprising designers have found ways around this obstacle, however. Ogbu cites the case of Busby Perkins+Will, a Canadian architecture firm that petitioned the city council of Vancouver to allow the reuse of plumbing and electrical elements on a project. Their argument was so persuasive that the council voted to amend the regulations. Structural engineers may also be resistant to the reuse of materials to form building structures. Ogbu's research found several solutions to this issue, from simply oversizing members to clearly exceeding building requirements to actually hiring a wood grader to assess beams and columns for their fitness for reuse. When 2012Architecten, a Rotterdam architecture practice dedicated to sustainable design, sought to reuse the steel components of a large industrial weaving machine to create a frame for Villa Welpeloo in Enschede (see page 102), their structural engineer cleverly based all design calculations on the lowest strength of steel.

As the knowledge base around material reuse grows, projects feature increasingly larger recycled elements. LOT-EK, a New York architecture practice founded by partners Giuseppe Lignano and Ada Tolla, has made a career out of appropriating some of the supersized components of our global industrial complex – objects like the shipping containers that have become the firm's trademark, aeroplane fuselages, water towers, truck trailers and road boxes, converting them into habitable spaces and buildings. Although sustainability is important to LOT-EK's work, it isn't the sole driver. 'Of course there's a sustainable point of view,' says Lignano, 'but there's also an artistic or political point of view. Somehow our culture is ashamed of all these things we produce. But we try to recognize their beauty and strength – to see them as something to play with and to use again.' The firm's careful transformations leverage the structural and material properties of salvaged materials into stunning contemporary buildings. LOT-EK's practice revolves around surveying the built environment, especially in industrial areas like ports and harbours, and maintaining a constant inventory of these types of objects from which to draw upon. This act of surveying and documenting is itself a project, which the outfit calls Urban Scan; the results were published as a book two years ago. 'We recycle the material, the energy and the intelligence behind these objects, which is often completely anonymous,' says Lignano. 'These objects are incredibly well designed but so utilitarian that you wouldn't realize it without studying them.'

Taking advantage of that in-built design thinking to repurpose an object is what Jan Jongert, a principal at 2012Architecten, refers to as 'super-use'. As opposed to reuse, super-use 'looks at a component or material and tries to find a new possibility that it hasn't had before', explains Jongert. In terms of environmental impact, reuse and super-use may be comparable, but in the transformation he refers to (one example is the cladding developed for Villa Welpeloo) the aesthetic and physical properties of the material are heightened in a new form, which may ultimately enhance awareness of the element's prior life. ■

'Working with locally sourced salvaged materials can help retain the cultural or social narrative of the community'
Liz Ogbu

The scale of the project made it feasible for a one-person design team

BLOODWOOD RESTAURANT & BAR

When three breakaway chefs from Claude, a fine-dining establishment in Sydney, decided to open an eatery in the up-and-coming suburb of Newtown, a natural choice for interior designer was Newtown-based Matt Woods, who shared their vision of a colourful, character-filled space built sustainably to reflect a menu based on minimum waste and seasonal produce.

The restaurant's commitment to reuse starts at the sign, which is fashioned from half a wood door, hinting at a motif that continues inside, where several more salvaged doors are layered to form an acoustic ceiling in the dining room. Still others adorn the back patio. The majority of the furniture specified for the project was reclaimed, including reupholstered stools and refurbished chairs.

Built-in elements are constructed primarily from salvaged and reclaimed timber, including a bar near the entrance consisting of several repurposed railway sleepers, a Sydney-style touch that Woods says goes back to his childhood, when it was common to find retaining walls in the garden crafted from railway sleepers. The scale of the project meant that customization and time spent sourcing objects for the interior were feasible for a one-person design team. ▬

DESIGNER Matt Woods (killingmattwoods.com)
DESCRIPTION Restaurant
LOCATION Newtown, Sydney, Australia
COMPLETED Spring 2010
REUSED Doors (ceiling and wall finishes), salvaged wood (bar and seating) and second-hand furniture

'We're interested in the longevity of things; this strategy represents not just an environmental point of view, but a larger architectural approach to problem solving'
Kevin Carmody

STUDIO EAST DINING

Summer saw an exotic visitor to the sprawling East London construction site for the 2012 Olympic Games: a temporary outpost of famous restaurant Bistrotheque. Called Studio East Dining, it appeared virtually out of thin air on the roof of a partially completed parking garage.

Approached by the owners to design a home for the temporary restaurant, Carmody Groarke immediately opted to make use of the many materials available nearby. Scaffolding from the construction site created the backbone of the project: several dining halls orientated around key views were combined to form an open pavilion. Salvaged timber lined inner walls supported by a steel skeleton, and boards from the construction site served as dining tables. Industrial lighting – caged for safety – was also 'borrowed' from the site. In fact, the only component that could not be dismantled and returned intact (or re-reused) was the heat-shrinkable EnviroWrap™ roof. Principal Kevin Carmody says the project was in keeping with the firm's policy: 'We're interested in the longevity of things; things are designed for a certain time frame or life span. This strategy represents not just an environmental point of view but a larger architectural approach to problem solving.'

Carmody Groarke took great care in designing proportions that would minimize the need for reduction (and waste) and maximize the potential for further reuse. 'We only had to resize pieces in the acute angles of the structure, in one or two instances where the junctions had to meet,' says Carmody. 'Overall, that was an absolutely minute amount of customization.' ∎

DESIGNER Carmody Groarke (carmodygroarke.com)
DESCRIPTION Temporary restaurant
LOCATION London, United Kingdom
COMPLETED June 2010
REUSED 'Borrowed' scaffolding, planks and lighting

'As you find the right pieces, you discover the path you have to take'
Fabrice Aeberhard

SALVAGED FURNITURE WAS ADAPTED TO CREATE COMPLEX
DISPLAY UNITS, ALL OF WHICH FORM A HARMONIOUS ENTITY,
THANKS TO UNIFORM SURFACES OF BLACK MDF.
PHOTOS NICO SCHAERER

KOMPLEMENTAIR ACCESSOIRES

When the owner of Komplementair Accessoires visited Café Z Am Park in Zurich, designed by Aekae, she knew she had found the right designers for her premier boutique. 'What appealed to her was the combination of old and new,' says Aekae cofounder Christian Kaegi. 'It was something she had in mind before she started.'

Reuse was part of the project from the beginning, from the space itself – located in a historical viaduct in Zurich – to the owner's request that Aekae include a cherished Steinway piano in the design. 'Our idea was to combine different pieces of furniture within bigger structures,' says Kaegi. 'The owner didn't want the merchandise to be grouped in categories; she wanted to show outfits and different pieces that matched well. Her request cast a new light on presentation.' Kaegi and partner Fabrice Aeberhard responded with an interior featuring assemblages of second-hand furniture: stacked, customized and fitted together to form display units. They gave each piece a custom-cut surface of black MDF, a unifying element that also referred to the piano. Working with found objects was 'both a challenge and an adventure' for the designers. 'As you find the right pieces,' says Aeberhard, 'you discover the path you have to take.' ■

DESIGNER Aekae (aekae.com)
DESCRIPTION Shop for men's and women's accessories
LOCATION Zurich, Switzerland
COMPLETED April 2010
CARPENTRY GregoryClan
IDENTITY Fabian Leuenberger
REUSED Salvaged and second-hand furniture

'It's important to add humour, which isn't often connected with green building'
Jan Jongert

REUSED MATERIALS HELP TO HUMANIZE
AN OTHERWISE MINIMALIST SPACE.
PHOTOS ALLARD VAN DER HOEK

VILLA WELPELOO & BAR

The flagship project of 2012Architecten, Villa Welpeloo, is a textbook example of what the firm calls 'super-use', the application of reclaimed materials for purposes other than those for which they were designed. Principal Jan Jongert estimates that 60 per cent of the project's materials are super-used (building regulations prohibited the use of recycled concrete for the foundations, or it would have been closer to 100 per cent).

2012Architecten begins every project by creating a 'harvest map', which identifies local sources of reusable materials. In the case of Villa Welpeloo, an industrial loom from a defunct textile manufacturer nearby yielded steel members for the main frame of the building (reducing carbon emissions by an estimated 95 per cent in comparison with the use of new steel). Secondary structure, roof, flooring and insulation were salvaged from local buildings slated for demolition. The cores of large wooden cable reels form the home's signature exterior cladding. 'Because they were taken from round cable reels, all the boards were slightly curved,' says Jongert. 'This gives the cladding a unique expression.'

The interior elements are no less innovative. What appears at first glance to be a stark, white, minimalist space (designed to showcase the clients' art collection) actually contains many playful touches: construction-site signage has become drawers and cabinetry, light fixtures are crafted from umbrellas, and recycled plastic materials have reappeared in the bathrooms. 'We think it's important to include humour in our work,' says Jongert. 'That's not something that is often connected with green building.' ■

DESIGNER 2012Architecten (2012architecten.nl)
DESCRIPTION Residence
LOCATION Enschede, the Netherlands
COMPLETED 2009
REUSED Industrial machinery (steel frame), reclaimed timber and insulation, construction signage (cabinetry) and umbrellas (light fixtures)

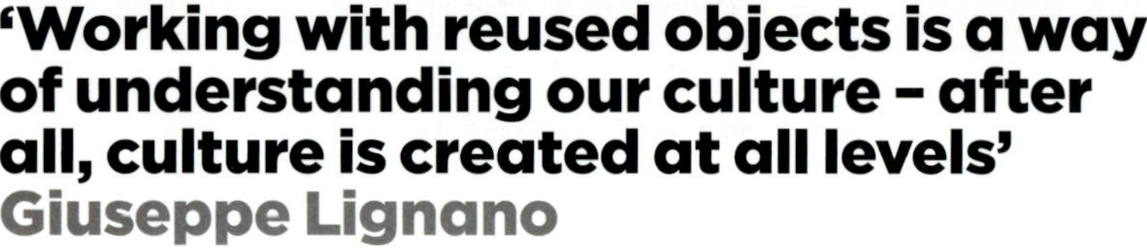

'Working with reused objects is a way of understanding our culture – after all, culture is created at all levels'
Giuseppe Lignano

EIGHT SHIPPING CONTAINERS
WERE SLICED AND SPLICED TO
CREATE AN ENIGMATICALLY
ANGULAR BUILDING.
PHOTOS SERGIO PIRRONE

APAP OPEN SCHOOL

'What's the line between learning from an object, understanding an object and taking advantage of an object – playing with it, breaking it and making it do things it doesn't want to do?' muses Giuseppe Lignano of New York-based LOT-EK. In this case, the object in question is the standard steel shipping container often used by the architecture firm as a building block.

Eight such containers were sliced and spliced to form the APAP (Anyang Public Art Project) Open School in South Korea. Perched on a riverbank, the building houses an exhibition space, offices and two artist-in-residence studios. These are lifted off the ground to provide shelter for an amphitheatre below. The two frontal walls are pierced with peepholes at different heights (for children as well as adults), framing views of nature and the surrounding urban context.

While the marriage between the industrial materials and the cultural programme might seem unlikely, for LOT-EK it makes perfect sense. 'Working with these objects is a way of understanding our culture,' says Lignano. 'After all, culture is created at all levels.' ▬

DESIGNER LOT-EK (lot-ek.com)
DESCRIPTION Riverside public amphitheatre and gallery
LOCATION Anyang, Korea
COMPLETED July 2010
REUSED Shipping containers

THE FORMER HEADQUARTERS OF THE IMPERIAL JAPANESE ARMY, BUILT IN THE 1930S, NOW ACCOMMODATE THE WATERHOUSE, A FOUR-FLOOR BOUTIQUE HOTEL IN THE SOUTH BUND DISTRICT.

SHANGHAI STORY

THE WATERHOUSE HOTEL is NHDRO's attempt to blur the boundaries between private and public, between old and new, and thus to reveal the essence of Shanghai.

WORDS **ALEXANDRA ONDERWATER**
PHOTOS **PEDRO PEGENAUTE**

CORRIDORS INSIDE THE HOTEL ALLOW GUESTS TO CATCH A GLIMPSE OF WHAT'S COMING NEXT.

NHDRO ENLARGED THE ENTRANCE, WHICH NOW WELCOMES GUESTS THROUGH A DOOR IN ONE CORNER OF A TALL WOODEN 'INSET' THAT INCLUDES AN OVERHANG.

'If you want to understand what makes Shanghai spin, this is the place to be'
Lyndon Neri

Anyone who's ever been to Shanghai is sure to have visited the Bund, the famous strip that, like everything else in the 'new' China, is the epitome of spaciousness. The broad promenade meanders along the west bank of the 400-m-wide Huangpu (literally 'yellow bank') River, which splits the immense port city into Puxi, home of the Bund, and its modern counterpart on the east bank, the fashionable Pudong. The Bund – a fusion of Champs-Élysées, Fifth Avenue and Copacabana – features Art-Deco crown jewels such as the Peace Hotel, the HSBC Building and the Bank of China, as well as less conspicuous hipster spots, design shops, glamorous restaurants and trendy clubs. In recent years, however, most of the attention has been aimed at the other side of the river, Pudong, where towering buildings and architectural tours

de force exert their magnetic pull on both locals and tourists, especially after the sun has set.

So where do you start? Do you zip straight up to Cloud 9, a hotel bar on the east bank, where a gaping hole at the top of the austerely designed building guarantees you a place among the stars? Or do you opt for the authentic tour and explore the old city to the west?

If it were up to architect Lyndon Neri, he'd have us *look* at Pudong, one of the many faces of the 'new' Shanghai, and *stay* in the historical part of town. In fact, he'd recommend accommodation at The Waterhouse at South Bund, a 19-room boutique hotel in a section of old Shanghai that appears to be the victim of a mad rush of development, to the horror of Lyndon Neri, a native of the Philippines who's been living in Shanghai for years. Neri has a mission for the

city to which he's pledged his heart. He fears the intrusion of the umpteenth entrepreneur from Hong Kong determined to erect one high-rise apartment building after another in Shanghai at the expense of public space. And it's precisely the 'blurriness' between public and private space, says Neri, that makes Shanghai so unique.

While scouting the area for a home for The Waterhouse, an observant Neri spied a rather run-down building at the south end of the Bund. It's here that ocean steamers once put into the port city and where freight was loaded and unloaded on Shanghai's docks. 'If you want to see the tallest tower, stay at a comfortable hotel with all the amenities and eat in the best restaurant, this is not the hotel for you,' Neri points out. 'But if you want to understand what Shanghai really is, what makes it spin, what >>>

THE ARCHITECTURAL CONCEPT IS BASED ON A SHARP
CONTRAST BETWEEN OLD AND NEW. IN THE LOBBY,
THE ORIGINAL WALLS WERE LEFT LARGELY INTACT.
PHOTO DERRYCK MENERE

'The notion of private versus public is constantly present'
Lyndon Neri

EXPOSURE CHARACTERIZES THE WATERHOUSE,
WHERE SIGHTLINES CONNECT BEDROOM
TO BATHROOM, BATHROOM TO BALCONY,
BALCONY TO RESTAURANT, AND SO FORTH.
PHOTO DERRYCK MENERE

THE CONTRAST BETWEEN OLD AND NEW MARKS NOT ONLY THE HOTEL INTERIOR BUT ALSO THE NEARBY SURROUNDINGS.
PHOTO TUOMAS UISHEIMO

PHOTO DERRYCK MENERE

ROOMS ARE FURNISHED WITH PIECES BY MOOOI, MAGIS, VITRA AND B&B, AMONG OTHERS, COMBINED WITH A SELECTION OF VINTAGE FURNITURE.

the intangible blur between domestic and public space feels like, then this is the place to be.'

Let's leave Neri's 'blur' for later. First the building. By Shanghai standards, The Waterhouse at South Bund is a remarkable structure. Not particularly tall – you can peek inside from street level (quite unusual in a city where virtually everything happens on the tenth, twentieth or thirtieth floor) – it turns the corner with an organic sweep. Particularly striking, when viewed from the waterside, are the very large windows high on the façade. Like enormous eyes, they stare unflinchingly across the water, challenging the posh half of the city. This bold gaze reminds us that The Waterhouse served as the former headquarters of the Imperial Japanese Army in the 1930s. For Neri, the contrast between old and new, between past

and future, is elementary. He reinforced the original concrete skeleton with armour of steel but left the concrete exposed as a reference to the area's industrial past. Neri's credo can be summed up in three words: context, context, context. The discerning visitor discovers in every peeling wall and every narrow stairwell a chapter from a history book.

For that matter, the stairs in this building tell a story all their own. In a city where the lift is an everyday fact of life, most guests have to get used to the ubiquitous presence of all these twisting, labyrinthine stairs ('I kept every single step'). To one degree or another, exposure characterizes The Waterhouse, thanks to features such as ingeniously designed footbridges, gigantic windows and floating glass floors. It's Neri's way of playing with the field of

tension between public and private space. 'You constantly see other people. There are sightlines from bathroom to bathroom, bathroom to balcony, balcony to restaurant, and so forth. The view of Pudong melts into the view of the garden. That intermingling, that blurriness, is what defines the Shanghai of today. But ten years from now it might be different. In most of the city's newer buildings, you walk from your personal lift straight into your living room. Communal space is on the way out. It's dangerous.' Corridor windows overlooking the dining room, public spaces that invite guests to peer into private rooms, private spaces that draw the eye to public environments – it's all for a reason. 'We cannot be without community, without other people. We exist through togetherness. This is the boutique hotel in a nutshell. I have been trying to explore the >>>

PHOTO DERRYCK MENERE

Neri's credo can be summed up in three words: context, context, context

MIRRORS ON THE INNER SURFACES OF WOODEN SHUTTERS THAT OPEN TO THE COURTYARD REINFORCE THE RELATIONSHIP BETWEEN INSIDE AND OUTSIDE.

essence of what Shanghai really is.' Despite the serious undertone of his remarks, Neri stresses the fun and the element of surprise that enliven this concept of 'openness'.

Together with wife and business partner Rosanna Hu, Neri heads the Neri & Hu Design and Research Office (NHDRO), a middle-size design and architecture agency. The couple also runs Design Republic, a small store-cum-showroom that carries the outfit's own products, as well as those of international brands, such as Vitra, Established & Sons and Moooi. The offices of both companies recently moved into a building in the former French Concession, where venerable architecture, including a great many low-rise buildings, recalls the former French presence in the city, and street vendors prepare and sell food. (During a slow spell, I even spotted one woman having her hair dyed.) In other parts of the city, the situation is quite different.

Obviously enjoying himself, Neri points to a place above our heads, where a guest crosses a glazed footbridge on the way to his hotel room. Although he can't hear us talking – or hear anything going on outside – he glances down and notices us looking at him. 'This notion of private versus public is constantly present. Is it really private? Is it really public? Am I safe? That sort of intensity is China – the notion of Big Brother watching you.' We take the stairs to the top level, where a rooftop bar provides a view of the new Shanghai across the river. If anything, The Waterhouse is a human gallery filled with ever-evolving works of art. ■■■■

THE WATERHOUSE AT SOUTH BUND

LOCATION Maojiayuan Road No. 1-3, Huangpu District, 200011, Shanghai, China
DESIGNER NHDRO (nhdro.com)
CLIENT Cameron Holdings Hotel Management Limited
AREA 2800 m²
MATERIALS Plaster, concrete, Corten steel, brick, recycled wood, glass, oak (floors)
FURNITURE Moooi, Tom Dixon, Magis, Fontana Arte, Vitra, Neri & Hu, B&B and vintage pieces
LIGHTING Moooi, Tom Dixon, Fontana Arte, Vitra
FLOOR MANUFACTURER Imondi
COMPLETED May 2010

NHDRO ADDED A FOURTH FLOOR TO THE
BUILDING: MADE FROM CORTEN STEEL,
THIS EXTENSION REFERENCES THE
INDUSTRIAL NATURE OF THE RIVERFRONT
AND THE SHIPS IN THE PORT.
PHOTO DERRYCK MENERE

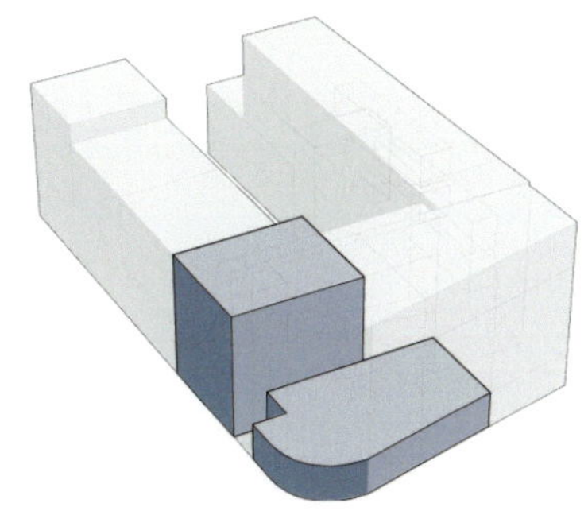

ARRIVAL AREAS: RECEPTION, LOUNGE AND BAR.

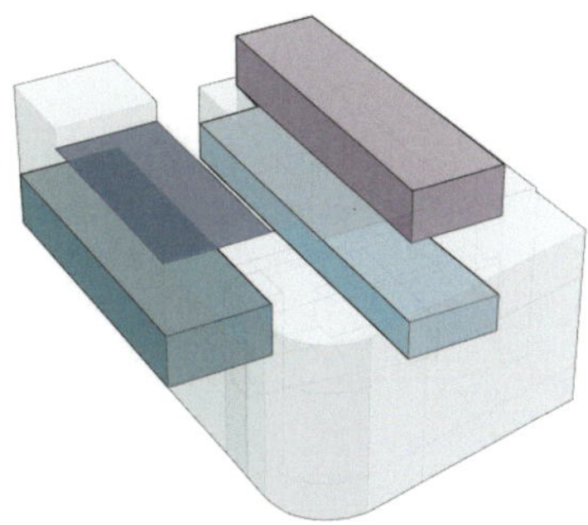

PUBLIC AREAS: RESTAURANT, KITCHEN, LIBRARY-CUM-LOUNGE AND ROOFTOP BAR.

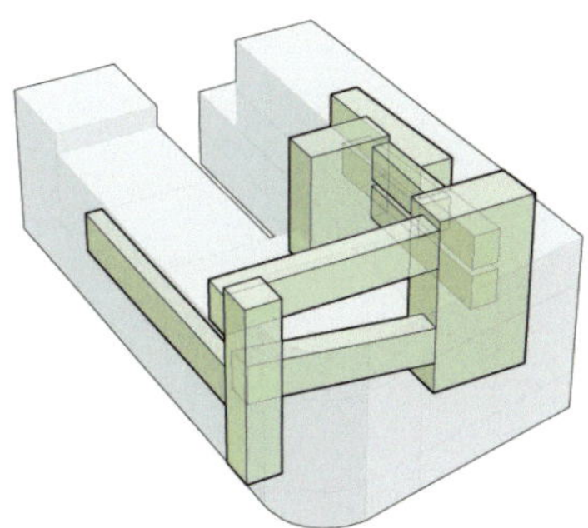

PUBLIC CIRCULATION: INTERIOR AND EXTERIOR CORRIDORS.

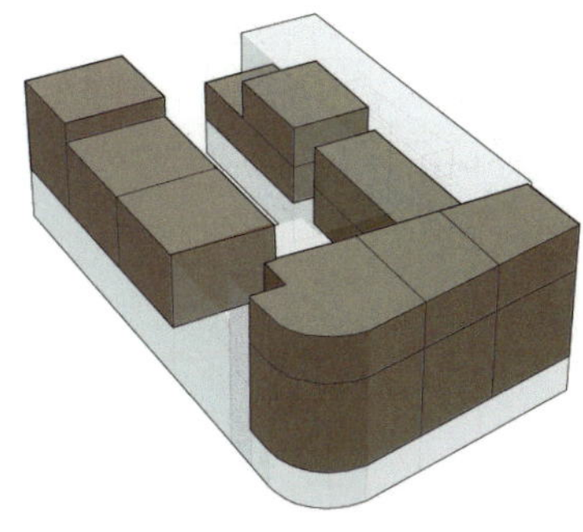

BLOCKS OF HOTEL ROOMS: NINE WITH COURTYARD VIEW, SEVEN WITH RIVER VIEW.

LONGITUDINAL SECTION.

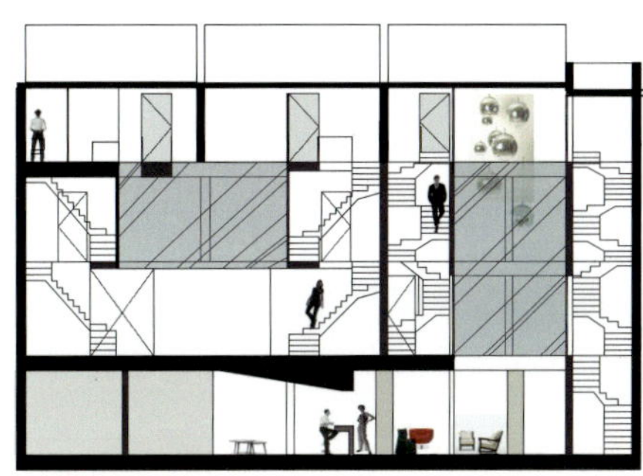

CROSS SECTION.

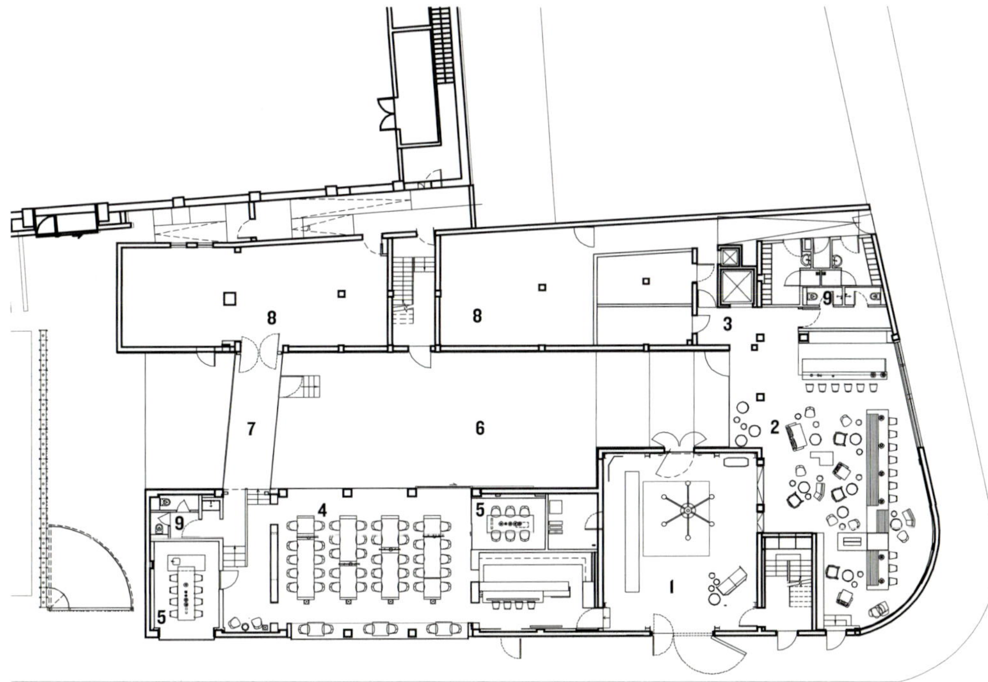

FIRST FLOOR.

1. LOBBY
2. LOUNGE
3. LIFT LOBBY
4. RESTAURANT
5. PRIVATE DINING ROOM
6. COURTYARD
7. CORRIDOR
8. KITCHEN
9. TOILET

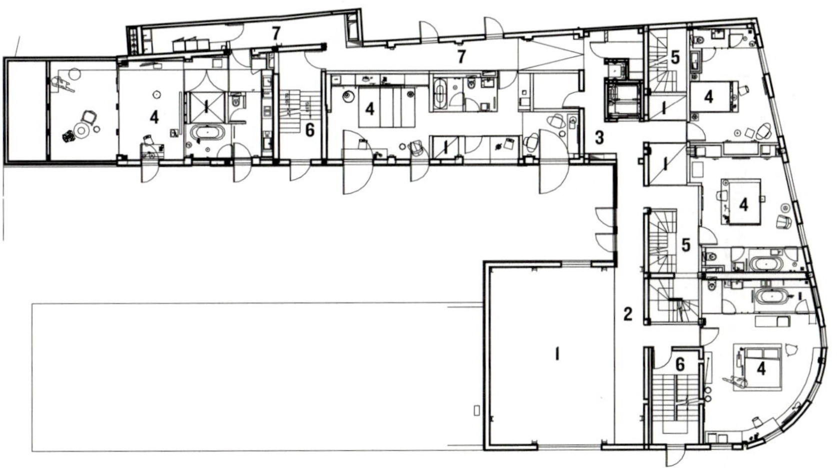

THIRD FLOOR.

1. VOID
2. FOOTBRIDGE
3. LIFT LOBBY
4. ROOM
5. STAIRS
6. FIRE EXIT STAIRS
7. CORRIDOR

ROBUST

Like a good wine that gets better with age, the OLARRA WINERY's 40-year-old premises gain a rich new flavour thanks to IA+B's burgundy glass.

WORDS **SUZANNE WALES**
PHOTOS **AITOR ORTIZ**

IA+B'S INTERVENTION WAS DICTATED BY THE ARRANGEMENT OF THE EXISTING STRUCTURAL DETAILS.

La Rioja has been Spain's largest and most productive wine region since the time of the Romans. Despite this fact, wine tourism has only really been established in the area over the past decade, as producers have commissioned major architects to build ambitious, showcase bodegas (wineries) and visitor's centres. The first was Santiago Calatrava's undulating Ysios winery, followed by Frank Gehry's City of Wine for the prestigious Marques de Riscal group. Other architects who have left their mark amid the vineyards of La Rioja and neighbouring Navarra include Zaha Hadid (for the López de Heredia), Rafael Moneo (Señorío de Chivite) and Iñaki Aspizau, with his ultra-modern Bodegas Baigorri. The Bilbao-based architecture studio IA+B is the latest to add its signature to the region.

Located on the outskirts of Logroño, the capital of the La Rioja, the Olarra bodega is situated in a massive Y-shaped, low-rise, concrete structure from the early 1970s. Rather than trying to compete with such an imposing and powerful presence, the architects decided to add a playful element to evoke the rich colour, taste and aroma of wine. The intervention has taken place in the existing atrium, where the arms of the Y meet and where an intricate arrangement of roof beams and rafters, columns, skylights, dormer windows and other elements dictated the direction of the project. 'This is a very unique structure. From the outset we decided that it shouldn't be touched,' says architect Josep Egea of IA+B. 'We then worked in 3D, as we found out early on that flat plans just weren't appropriate for this project.'

The most striking aspect of IA+B's work is the abundant laminated glass surfaces in the same deep red as La Rioja's famous tempranillo grape, adding a palpable depth and distinctive light to the intervention. (The studio employed laminated glass equally as effectively in Bilbao's acclaimed Hotel Hesperia). Arranged into block-like rectangular volumes, the panels are held in place by a network of black supports, echoing the hexagonal geometry of the atrium.

The ground floor, which contains an exhibition space and retail area, has been covered in oak, a popular material in contemporary wine architecture because of its reference to the winemaking process. Other elements in this section – such as benches and display stands – have been conceived in the same material, lending an organic touch to the project. From here, visitors can access the upper floor via an elegant, floating staircase located at its axis and placed inside the glassed-in area. Upstairs there is a tasting area, a conference room (with a startling view over the exterior of the roof of the bodega's ageing rooms with its 111 domes) and new offices, while the ground floor can be viewed through the transparent volumes, much like looking through the bottom of a glass of wine.

All of the elements in the project were manufactured locally and then built on site. 'Cost-wise, this project was not expensive,' affirms Egea. 'It wasn't an easy task and we tried several things before we got it right. The result may look complex, but actually it's very simple.' ■

THE OLARRA BODEGA IS SITUATED IN A
Y-SHAPED, LOW-RISE, CONCRETE STRUCTURE
FROM THE EARLY 1970S.

GLASS SURFACES IN THE SAME RED AS LA
RIOJA'S FAMOUS TEMPRANILLO GRAPE ADD
DEPTH AND LIGHT TO THE EXISTING SPACE.

THE GROUND FLOOR HOUSES AN EXHIBITION SPACE AND RETAIL AREA, AND HAS BEEN COVERED IN OAK IN REFERENCE TO THE WINEMAKING PROCESS.

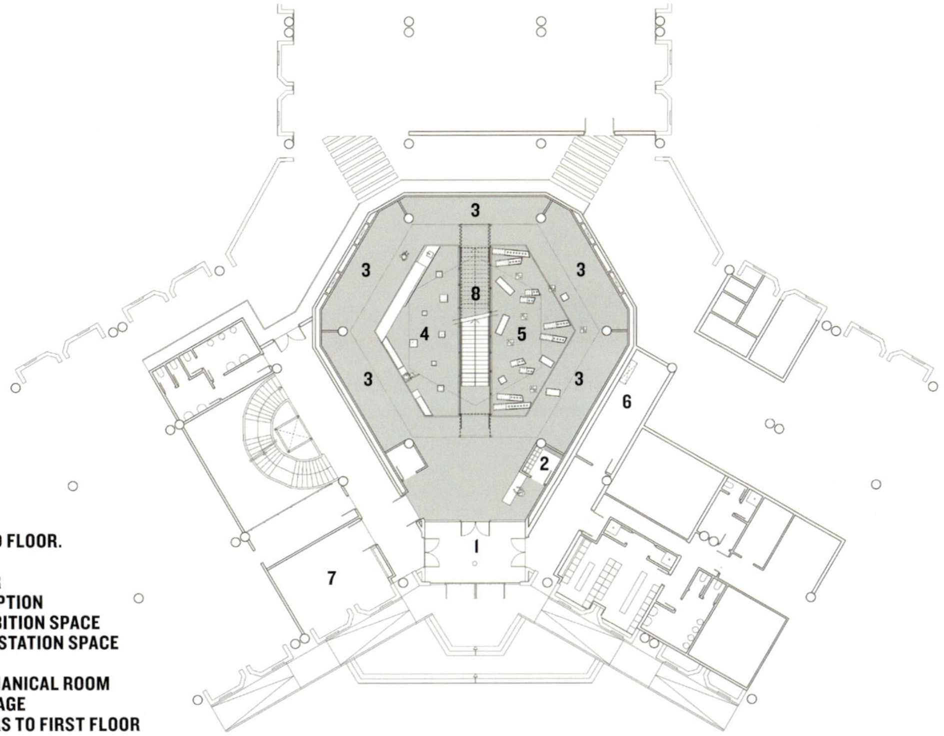

GROUND FLOOR.

1. FOYER
2. RECEPTION
3. EXHIBITION SPACE
4. DEGUSTATION SPACE
5. SHOP
6. MECHANICAL ROOM
7. STORAGE
8. STAIRS TO FIRST FLOOR

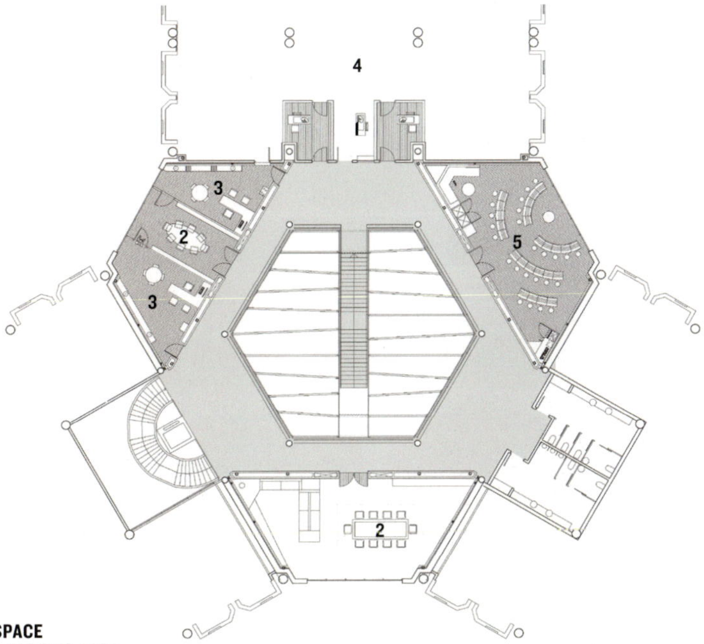

FIRST FLOOR.

1. RECEPTION
2. MEETING ROOM
3. OFFICE
4. OPEN-PLAN OFFICE SPACE
5. PROFESSIONAL WINE TASTING AREA

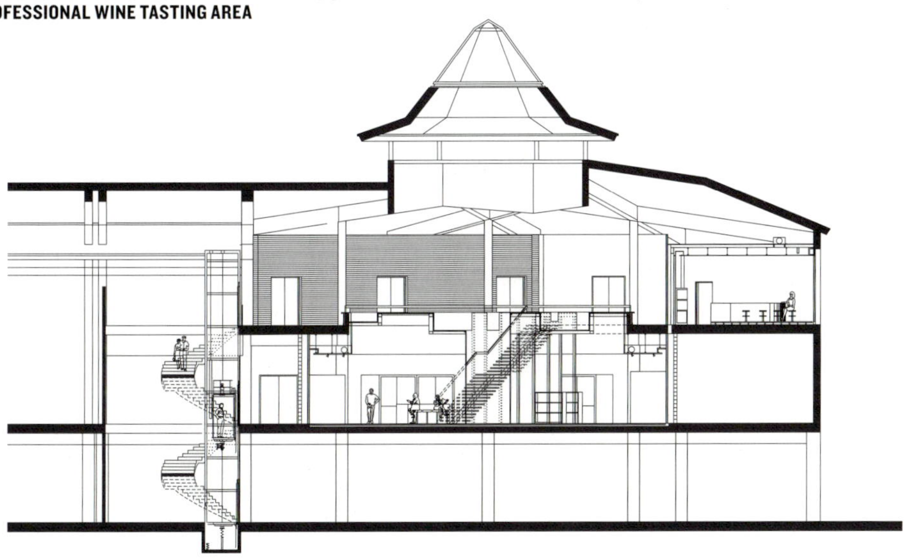

SECTION LOOKING SOUTH-EAST.

'The result may look complex, but actually it's very simple'
Josep Egea

BODEGAS OLARRA

LOCATION Avda. De Mendavia 30, 26006 Logroño, Spain
DESIGNER IA+B (iab-arkitek.com)
CLIENT Bodegas Olarra
AREA 1066 m²
BUDGET € 1,285,000
COMPLETED May 2010

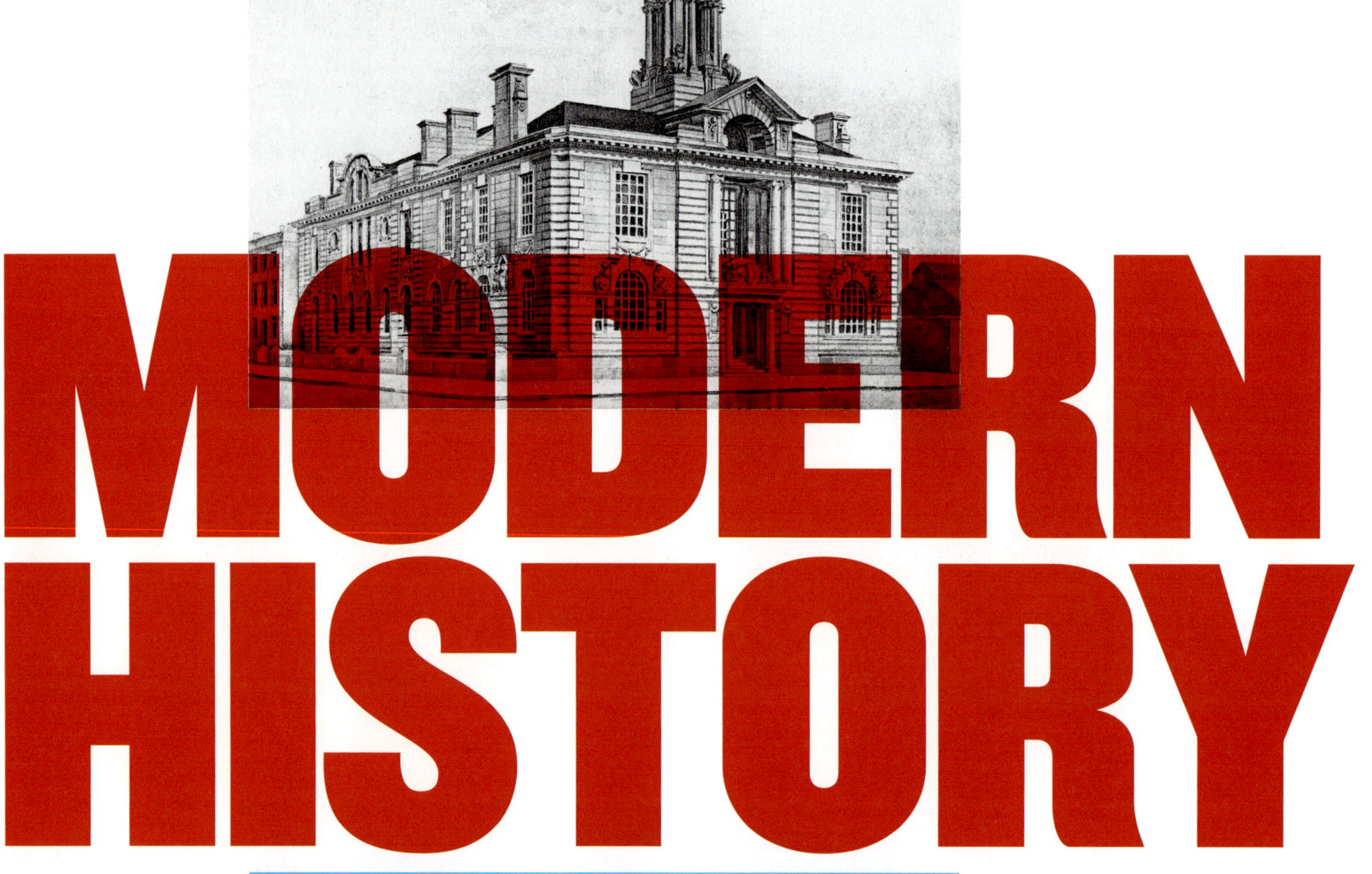

MODERN HISTORY

In London's East End, RARE ARCHITECTURE has transformed a protected, early 20th-century town hall into a dramatically contemporary hotel – without losing anything of the past.

WORDS **GIOVANNA DUNMALL**
PHOTOS **EDMUND SUMNER, COURTESY OF RARE ARCHITECTURE**

THE EXTENSION AND A NEW STOREY HAVE BEEN WRAPPED IN A LASER-CUT, POWDERED ALUMINIUM SKIN – INSPIRED BY ART DECO GRATINGS IN THE ORIGINAL BUILDING.

It may not be located in the likeliest of settings, but that is part of the idiosyncratic charm of Town Hall Hotel & Apartments. This new design hotel in London's East End overlooks council housing on two sides and is steps away from the fast-food joints, often dingy pubs and neon-lit 24-hour minimarts of Bethnal Green Road. Gentrification has made huge strides in neighbouring trendy Shoreditch and Hoxton to the northwest, yet this particular pocket of Bethnal Green remains, rather refreshingly, neglected and impervious.

As its name suggests, the hotel is housed in what was a town hall from Edwardian times right up until it fell into disuse, along with many other local town halls, in the early 1990s. A listed monument, it languished for a good 15 years before reaching a state of disrepair, its abandonment relieved only occasionally when the site appeared as an atmospheric backdrop in films such as *Atonement*. Enter 30-something Singaporean lawyer and hotelier Loh Lik Peng in 2006, a man with a passion for historical buildings and a penchant for designer and vintage chairs of the 1950s and 1960s. He promptly bought the building and put Paris- and London-based practice Rare Architecture on the roster to restore, renovate and expand the complex, as well as to design all interior furnishings. Rare may be small and young, but these architects were serious, had done their research (poring over original plans and photos found in local libraries) and were, according to the entrepreneur, über-knowledgeable. As far as Bethnal Green is concerned, it may not be as trendy as Shoreditch, but it is minutes from the city, well connected by tube and train, and slap bang in the middle of the Olympic action come 2012.

The town hall has two distinct parts: a fairly bombastic Edwardian block facing the main artery of Cambridge Heath Road, and a more classical 1930s expansion with many Art-Deco flourishes to the east that reoriented the building and gave it a new façade on a road misleadingly called Patriot Square (a square it ain't by any stretch of the imagination). The façades of both parts are cloaked in Portland stone, though most of the building is actually made of far cheaper brick. The complex was due to be expanded even farther east back in the 1930s – to make space for a ballroom, explains Michael da Costa Gonçalves, founding director of Rare, along with Nathalie Rozencwajg – and was supposed to look out onto a proper square (instead of the current squat and uninspiring council estate), but the war reared its head and expansion plans were forgotten.

It is only now, in 2010, or what Da Costa Gonçalves and Rozencwajg call the building's 'third age', that the building has finally been expanded and given an extra storey on its roof (which becomes two storeys along part of the lower 1910 structure) and a new lease of life. In total, the extension has added an extra 1500 m^2 to an existing structure of 7500 m^2. The extension and much of the south-facing part of the complex have been wrapped in a laser-cut, powder-coated aluminium skin with a modulated pattern (inspired by, among other things, the elegant Art-Deco grilles visible in the building's striking maple-panelled meeting rooms and the nearly intact 1930s council chamber) that filters the amount of light coming in, provides privacy for the rooms' occupants, and defines their view of the surroundings. >>>

'The idea was to edit the surroundings'
Michael da Costa Gonçalves

OLD COUNCIL CHAMBERS (TOP) AND MEETING ROOMS HAVE BEEN REFURBISHED AND GIVEN A NEW LEASE OF LIFE.

THE DE MONTFORD SUITE: 'OCCASIONALLY, THE IMPOSSIBLY HIGH-CEILINGED ROOMS SEEM NEITHER PROPERLY CONTEMPORARY NOR CONVINCINGLY ORIGINAL' – A CONSEQUENCE OF THE NEED TO LEAVE THE OLD FABRIC UNTOUCHED.

BATHROOMS AND KITCHENS PLAY WITH
VARIOUS KINDS OF WHITENESS, FROM OLD
MOULDINGS TO SLEEK CERAMICS.

Constraints have simply made this project better

ROOMS IN THE PRE-EXISTING BUILDING REVEAL A USUALLY HAPPY UNION BETWEEN OLD AND NEW, WITH LACQUERED KITCHEN UNITS AND CORIAN BATHROOM CUBES OFFSETTING THE PERIOD FEATURES.

This is where Da Costa Gonçalves becomes academic (he and Rozencwajg are both Architectural Association professors) and starts to talk about 'parameterized language', 'shaped grammar' and 'performative ornaments'. More simply he says: 'The idea was to edit the surroundings.' The skin 'creates a kind of distance; you feel protected from outside'.

What Rare hoped to achieve with its additions was a balancing of all the different styles that existed in the structure. The architects wanted to reorganize the building and make it work as a whole, including the various gaps and changes in levels between the two parts. 'The building is not a perfect example of anything,' says Da Costa Gonçalves. 'It's a beautiful building, but it is quite heterogeneous in style.' This explains why they created an entirely new façade at the back (the laser-cut cloak or veil referred to earlier), one they strived to make as interesting as the façade at the front but 'more contemporary'. Their aim was to overcome the idea of 'this is the front and this is the back', to make the complex work from all angles.

And it does work. From the outside, the bespoke skin is functional, sculptural and playful. It changes tone depending on the time of day. From the inside, it works as a tool for framing the outside, while letting in only as much of it as you want. Above the 1937 façade – and set back slightly from the original frontage – the veil moves in and out of sight according to the light and effectively erases any signs of the 'windows, doors or chimneys' of the rooftop extension, becoming an abstract, and at night atmospherically lit and enticing, signifier for what might lie behind.

What lies behind is just as interesting, fortunately, as the multiple façades. There is the grand entrance hall, with its columns and imposing marble staircase; 98 apartments and rooms; an intimate restaurant; a buzzy, glamorous bar filled with furniture designed by Rare and featuring a dramatic injected-silicone chandelier created by textile designer Tzuri Gueta; a Secession-inspired lap pool and mirror-filled gym; many former public spaces, including council chambers and meeting rooms, which have been restored and given a new lease of life; and even a glazed dome and a tower. The Art-Deco motif of the ventilation grilles is echoed in the rooms (all different and based on location), in particular in the CNC-milled patterns that have been cut into the solid, made-to-measure MDF units, which function not only as elegant partitions but also house wardrobes, kitchenettes and washing machines. Rare also used heavy sliding doors, which glide with ease into hidden spaces, and curtains to close off, define or open up the different areas of rooms and apartments. For Da Costa Gonçalves and Rozencwajg, the patterned MDF units represent an ideal combination of new technologies and craft. In one room, the kitchen is delineated by a carved MDF unit that has been left 'pure': the surface wears nothing but a simple coat of varnish. The piece is textured, multi-toned and unexpectedly fascinating and beautiful. 'We like the idea of this very poor material becoming exceptional because of the craft applied to it,' says a smiling Da Costa Gonçalves.

Rooms in the existing building reveal an often happy union between old and new, with period fireplaces, Crittall windows (sporting their original mechanisms, now refurbished >>>

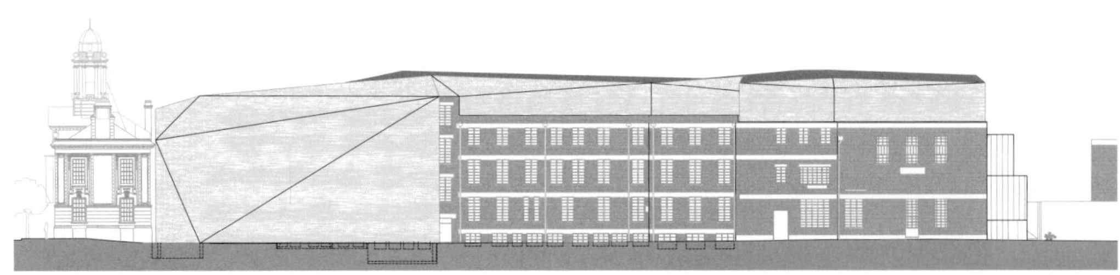

SOUTH ELEVATION: THE REAR OF THE BUILDING, SHOWING ITS FAÇADE 'SKIN'.

TOWN HALL HOTEL & APARTMENTS

LOCATION Patriot Square, E2 9NF London, UK
DESIGNER Rare architecture (r-are.net)
REUSED Existing buildings and original furnishings (lighting, windows) and furniture
COMPLETED April 2010

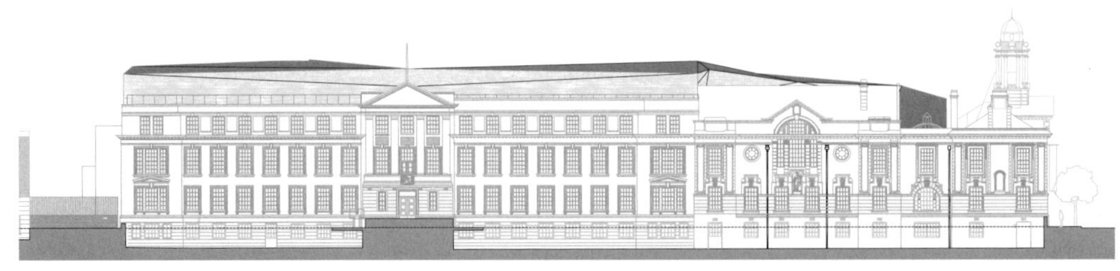

NORTH ELEVATION: THE FRONT VIEW, WITH THE FAÇADE SKIN VISIBLE ON THE ROOF.

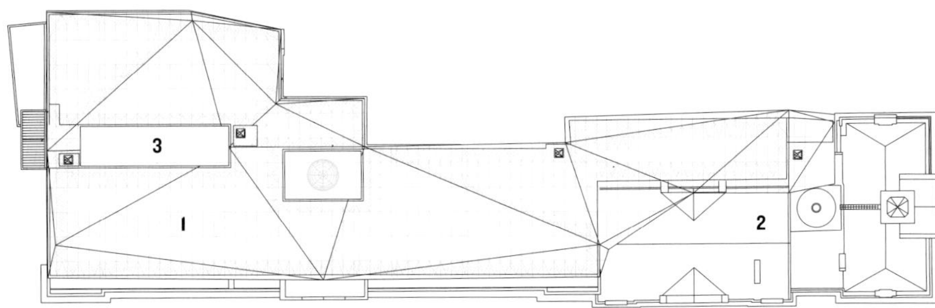

ROOF PLAN.

1. NEW 'SKIN' ROOF
2. ORIGINAL ROOFTOP
3. COURTYARD

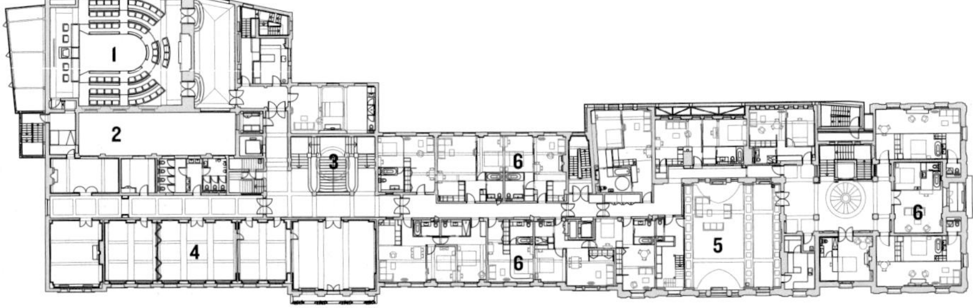

FIRST FLOOR.

1. CONFERENCE HALL
2. COURTYARD
3. STAIRS
4. MEETING ROOMS
5. DE MONTFORD SUITE
6. APARTMENTS

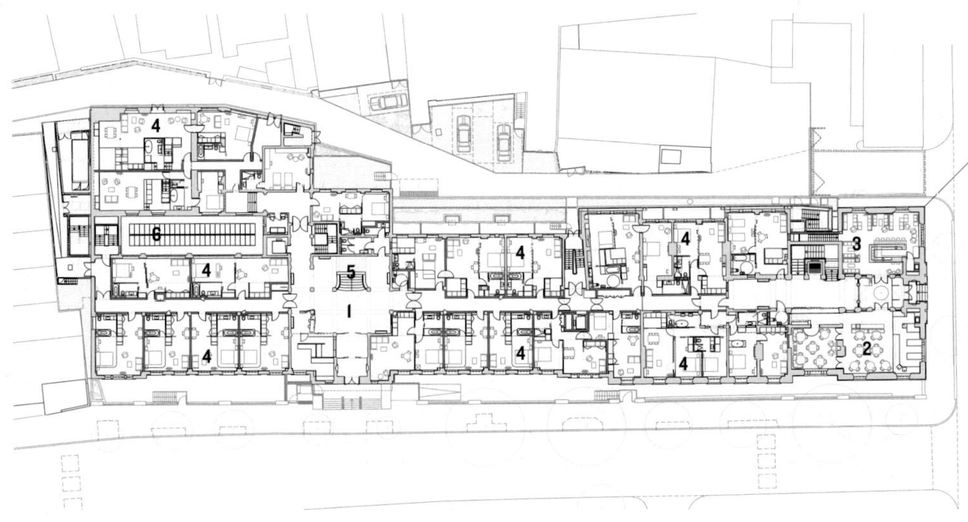

GROUND FLOOR.

1. ENTRANCE AND RECEPTION
2. RESTAURANT
3. BAR
4. APARTMENTS
5. STAIRS
6. COURTYARD

FACILITIES LIKE THE SECESSION-INSPIRED LAP POOL
CONTINUE THE GRANDIOSE, EVEN BOMBASTIC,
THEME OF THE ORIGINAL EDWARDIAN TOWN HALL.

and gleaming) and original furniture blending perfectly with the clean lines of white Corian cube bathrooms (themselves offset by green marble or grey Vals stone floors) and chic lacquered kitchen units. Even the technical elements, such as extractor fans and heating or air-conditioning equipment, are fitted into seamlessly designed slots that Da Costa Gonçalves says they have been asked to patent for future projects. Furniture found on the premises – such as benches, desks and chairs from the 1930s council chamber – has been refurbished and used in communal areas and in the breakfast room. But even in rooms devoid of original elements, the furniture is a combination of new and bespoke pieces designed by Rare, reproductions of period pieces and refurbished items (mostly Scandinavian) from the 1950s and 1960s.

The eras sit together in harmony for the most part, with rarely a faux pas. A couple of rooms in the oldest part of the building, especially the gigantic De Montfort Suite, suffer a little from Rare's extreme (and understandable) effort to leave the magnificent period interiors, accessories and mouldings intact. Da Costa Gonçalves says that since they couldn't add partitions or divisions to these rooms, they relied on 'spatial furniture', bedroom boxes and bathrooms to do the work. The contemporary insertions (bedrooms and bathroom on raised platforms or, in the suite, on several raised levels) remain just that, insertions. In the words of Da Costa Gonçalves: 'This allowed us to keep the room untouched.' In theory, he's saying that spatial elements can be taken out at any point, leaving the room as it was. The result is that the impossibly high-ceilinged rooms feel neither properly contemporary nor convincingly original, and the occupant feels half sassy urban sophisticate and half administrative official about to attend an urgent council meeting.

Elsewhere, constraints simply make the project better. An example is the 'double curvature' moulded ceiling found in the hallways of the lower-ground floor. Chosen because of its very low height (210 cm) and the need to install elements such as air-conditioning, the ceiling gives the corridors a flowingly sinuous and spacious feel. Also wholly successful is the first-floor room carved out of former ladies and gents toilets, where the outline in the terrazzo mosaic flooring of the cubicles is still visible. In the bathroom, Rare has used half-polished, half-matte mosaic tiles made out of marble. 'You get a glittering effect. It is white but not real white,' says Da Costa Gonçalves enigmatically. Earlier he had said that 'whites can be more than just white' when showing me the contrasts between various polar surfaces.

It is this level of detail and cultural and historical referencing, accompanied by technological input, that lifts the Town Hall Hotel out of the realm of being merely a sensitive restoration and into that of being an all-encompassing design project, from the 'shaped vocabulary' of the external skin to the suspended geometric lighting by Viabizzuno in every room, which creates 'elegant new proportions under the chaotic original beams of the ceilings'. As Da Costa Gonçalves mentions at one point, real simplicity is actually very difficult to achieve. This massive and unusual project deserves almighty praise for trying and, for the most part, succeeding in the attempt. ▬

THE FAÇADE FILTERS THE LIGHT, SHIELDS OCCUPANTS' PRIVACY, REFERS TO THE ART DECO STYLE OF THE ORIGINAL – AND CENSORS THE HOTELS NOT-YET-GENTRIFIED SURROUNDINGS.

THE ALUMINIUM SKIN UNIFIES THE BUILDING
AND OBLITERATES THE POLARITY BETWEEN
FRONT AND BACK.

THE DÉCOR OF THE EXHIBITION ABOUT CITY LIFE SHOWS
SKYSCRAPERS, SLUMS AND SHOPPING STREETS. SPORT,
CULTURE AND A CITY PARK CONVERGE ON LEISURE SQUARE.

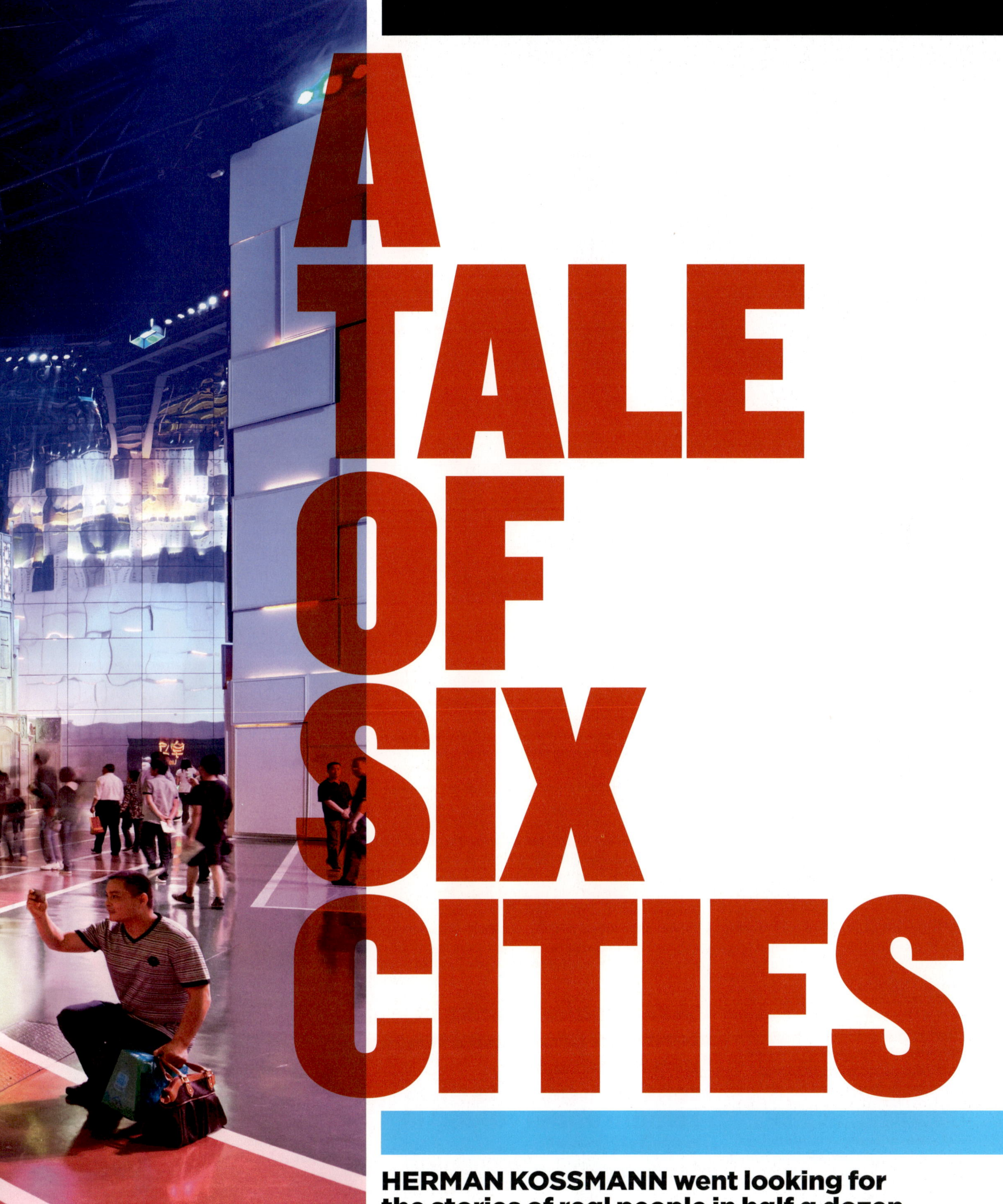

A TALE OF SIX CITIES

HERMAN KOSSMANN went looking for the stories of real people in half a dozen global metropolises for the URBANIAN PAVILION in Shanghai.

WORDS **FEMKE DE WILD**
PHOTOS **THIJS WOLZAK**

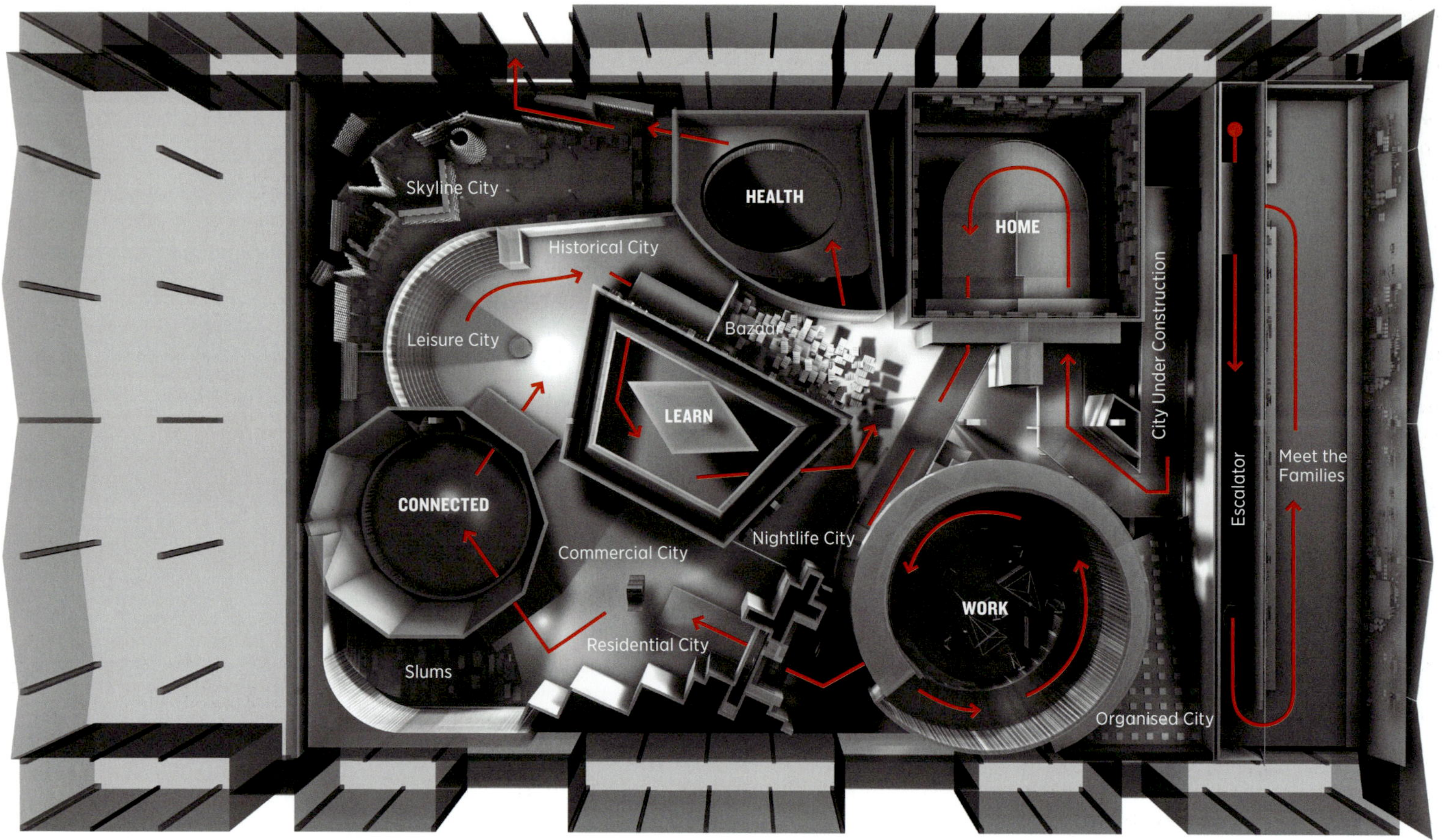

'A visit to an exhibition can be best compared to a tour of a city. You walk through a story, determine your own pace and use all your senses.' Herman Kossmann is sitting with senior designer Michèl de Vaan at a large conference table in the office of Kossmann.dejong, in the heart of Amsterdam, on the bank of the IJ inlet. Partner Mark de Jong gathers up sketches for the MicroZoo, a new project that will be a permanent feature of the local zoo, Artis, while Kossmann opens an enormous book about the World Expo in Shanghai. After a successful pitch – Kossmann.dejong was one of 150 firms competing for the commission, only 15 of which made the second round – the Amsterdam agency was asked to design the visual form and content of one of five Chinese pavilions. In this case, the design of the Urbanian Pavilion literally resembled a walk through the city.

'The pavilion had to be about life in a city, about people, and for us the focus was on a single question,' says Kossmann. 'What makes city life so attractive that it beckons one and all, that people even board a tiny boat and risk their lives to get to that city on the other side of the water?' After discussing the subject with a historian, an urban sociologist and a specialist in the field of new towns, the design agency came to the conclusion that five themes determine the quality of life in a city: housing, work, communication, education and health. The power of attraction exerted by each of these aspects lies in variation and supply. 'In a small village, you know well in advance how your life will evolve, what type of work you'll be doing and what kind of girl you'll marry,' says Kossmann. 'In the city, the possibilities are endless.'

Inside the gigantic pavilion – 150 by 100 m and a towering 22 m tall – a crew of 300 people built a metropolis out of everyday objects. An organized urban neighbourhood was made from milk cartons, while stacked crates became skyscrapers, removal boxes a skyline and corrugated cardboard a slum area. 'It didn't turn out exactly as we'd envisioned,' he says. 'China has an adventurous attitude, so there's not much you can't do, but when you make something in China, somehow or another it's always going to be Chinese. They like to reproduce everything as precisely as possible, even if it's supposed to look old. We wanted to allow room for imagination, though. It was a constant battle between the literal and the abstract. We spent a lot of time in Shanghai, but to have everything go perfectly – including construction – we should

'A filmmaker thinks in terms of protagonists, in a build-up of tension – aspects that remain undervalued in exhibitions'
Herman Kossmann

have moved there for the duration, as did John Körmeling, who designed the Dutch pavilion (see *Frame* 75, page 128).

The walk through the Urbanian Pavilion begins in the morning and takes visitors through five subpavilions, each comprising a separate

exhibition devoted to one of the chosen themes. An ingenious lighting plan and sound design create the illusion of a whole day passing in the 45 minutes needed to tour the building. The layout is unusual and is based on sightlines. As you walk through the commercial centre of town, bright with big neon signs, you see slum areas in the distance, and skyscrapers stand tall behind a low-rise urban neighbourhood. Brought in especially for this project was Matt Vermeulen, whose years of experience in theatrical set design made his input invaluable. 'In the meantime, Matt has become a permanent member of our team,' says Michèl de Vaan. 'It's one example of how our team grows increasingly stronger as people from all sorts of disciplines climb on board. We have lighting designers, architects and people like me, with a background in interactive technologies.'

Exhibiting has long been confined to the presentation of objects, but clients looking for no more than a handsome pedestal or an interesting display case to highlight an artefact needn't bother calling on Kossmann.dejong. 'We more or less hijack every commission,' says a grinning De Vaan. From the outset of each project, a multidisciplinary team is involved in developing the concept. Depending on the client, specialists are asked to furnish substantive input, and those directly involved in the concept phase include not only architects, but also lighting and sound designers. 'People from different disciplines offer different perspectives. Light and sound shouldn't be layers slapped on a design at a later date; everything should be integrated,' says Kossmann. During the development of a project, his role is more like that of a director than of a designer. 'There are enough designers,' he says. 'We always use content as the point of departure for our work. First we need a story, a scenario. Form isn't important; that comes automatically.'

Two filmmakers were part of the process that led to the exhibition in Shanghai. 'We wanted to show reality,' explains De Vaan. 'With unscripted images of real people, you can make abstract statistics pertaining to life in the city both personal and recognizable.' Six families were filmed, all leading ordinary lives in big cities, each on a different continent. Kossmann.dejong called this part of the project 'The Expedition'. Using the five earlier-mentioned themes, they made a series of 3.5-minute films – each family features in five short films – which became focal points of the subpavilions. Originally, the overall theme had been 'In Pursuit of Happiness', but it was soon changed to 'Quality of Life'. 'In China, balance is crucial,' says Kossmann. 'Happiness is too one-sided; furthermore, a large part of the population still lives in rural areas, and the city cannot be interpreted as a "better" place to be.'

Political sensitivity in host country China emerged again during the search for the right six families to film. The process was long and complicated: which cities to select and what kinds of families? 'If it had been up to us, the contrasts would have been much sharper,' says Kossmann. 'We wanted a millionaire from Moscow, someone from a São Paolo favela, and a Parisian artist. Paris was approved early on, or so it seemed until the Dalai Lama paid a visit to the city.' After many extensive and detailed presentations of the concept to a 40-member Chinese delegation, the choice finally fell on six very ordinary families. 'That's got its good side, too,' says Kossmann. 'It's easy for the visitor to identify with the main characters of the story.'

In Kossmann's opinion, few exhibitions take the opportunity to engage people and make them part of the theme in an optimal way. 'It's perfectly normal for a filmmaker to think in terms of protagonists, in a build-up of tension, in flashbacks – to use a scriptwriter and a sound designer. All this remains undervalued in most exhibitions. Allowing the visitor to stop in the middle of a story, or even to retrace his steps, can give an exhibition that extra jolt of excitement. By telling multiple stories simultaneously, you can make comparisons and encourage people to form associations on their own: impossible to do when staging plays or showing films. The potential is gigantic. You can tell important stories in a moving way to a very large audience. The World Expo could elaborate on such ideas much more than it does.'

The World Expo was initiated in the distant past for the purpose of exhibiting cultural, social and, in particular, technical developments. Nowadays, however, the event has turned into a series of billboards for the world's many nations. 'At an expo, you could examine serious subjects like energy, human rights and famine in a creative way,' Kossmann continues. 'The next World Expo will be held in Milan, where the main theme will be food. Why not have the following one in the middle of Africa, a continent that really needs the world to join forces and focus on food? It's a shame that the emphasis of most pavilions is on the architecture and that the story they want to tell is of minor importance. The best pavilions in history were *gesamtkunstwerken* in which great names combined a diversity of strengths. You can layer a variety of disciplines

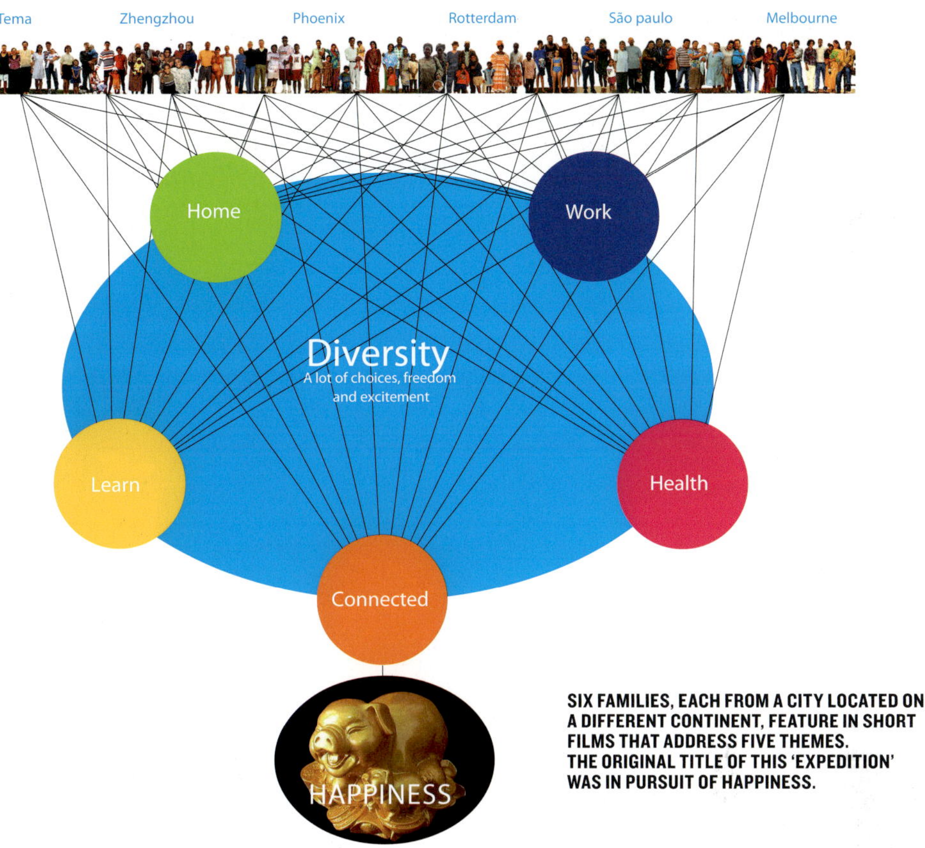

SIX FAMILIES, EACH FROM A CITY LOCATED ON A DIFFERENT CONTINENT, FEATURE IN SHORT FILMS THAT ADDRESS FIVE THEMES. THE ORIGINAL TITLE OF THIS 'EXPEDITION' WAS IN PURSUIT OF HAPPINESS.

ad infinitum, combine old and new technologies, and experiment endlessly. This is what makes our job so interesting.'

According to Kossmann, mixing disciplines can be applied more often and not only in exhibitions. Both Kossmann and De Jong were trained as architects, and in addition to exhibitions and permanent museum interiors, they design environments for hotels, restaurants and other public places. 'If more designers would realize that an interior is being made for people who will use it, and that these people are a sort of audience, they would produce much better work,' says Kossmann. 'I'd like to see a lot more thought given to the senses. Music can work really well in a home for the elderly, for example, as can elements that feel different, that stimulate the sense of touch. Too many designers think first and foremost of their own preferences.'

Besides interior design and an increasing number of requests from architects who want the agency to 'think along' with them on various projects, Kossmann.dejong sees exhibition design as the main player in its game plan. 'But we're talking here about exhibitions in which more and more often it won't be objects that tell the story,' says Kossmann. 'I love building a narrative out of nothing, putting a personal twist on a project, translating something from the past into the present, and imbuing the result with a sense of half knowing, half experiencing. It's an approach that invariably results in another interesting enterprise.' ■■■

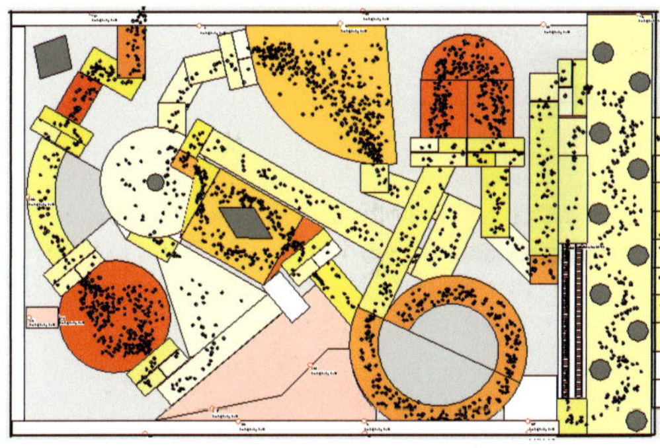

AN ANIMATION CREATED BY A CROWD-CONTROL CONSULTANT OPTIMIZE THE FLOW OF VISITORS, A GOAL THAT INFLUENCES SUCH MATTERS AS THE LENGTH OF THE FILMS AND THE WIDTH OF THE AISLES.

THE CITY

Every day, 40,000 visitors enter the pavilion via a 10-m-high escalator and make their first acquaintance with the six families. During their walk through the city, they pass five sub-pavilions where the sub-themes provide the central focus. In each of the pavilions – Home, Work, Connected, Learn and Health – videos of all six families can be seen on synchronized multiscreen projections. ■■■

MIRRORS ON THE CEILING AND FLOOR REFLECT
THE SPACE INTO INFINITY.

SHORT FILMS SHOW HOW MEMBERS OF THE VARIOUS FAMILIES (IN, FROM TOP TO BOTTOM, SÃO PAOLO, ROTTERDAM AND PHOENIX) GET UP IN THE MORNING AND CLEAN THEIR TEETH.

HOME

The pavilion consists of more than 120 show-boxes, an exhibition technique that has essentially been in use for centuries. On the screens, 3D images can be seen made from photos of various living rooms in the chosen cities. The largest boxes show film images of the six families simultaneously getting up, opening the curtains, brushing their teeth and eating. LED lamps, sound and video are all synchronized. Statistical facts and personal stories complement each other. ▰

HERMAN KOSSMANN (RIGHT) AND MICHÈL DE VAAN EVALUATE A MODEL OF THE MACHINE FOR THE WORK PAVILION.

WORK

Chinese Army engineers developed a large rotating machine for the Work pavilion where the central focus is dynamics. Videos of the six families can be seen on six large screens, which relate, for example, how many hours each main figure works per week. All sorts of details can be found on 22 rotating TFT screens. 

VISITORS CROSS A GRADUALLY SLOPING RAMP THAT SURROUNDS THE INSTALLATION. THE BARREL-SHAPED PAVILION HAS A DIAMETER OF 30 M.

THE FILM IN THE 'CONNECTED' PAVILION INCLUDES PEOPLE ON THE PHONE, METRO MAPS AND DIAGRAMS OF SOCIAL NETWORKS.

CONNECTED

There are no individual films to be seen in this pavilion, but eight beamers project consecutive images onto the domed roof. To begin with, Kossmann.dejong wanted to make a network of vertically and diagonally stretched strings that visitors literally had to walk through, but that was not feasible, for logistic reasons. In the end, an 8-m-high horizontally suspended woven construction refers to the concept and importance of social networks, transport systems and meeting places. ▬

TEENAGERS CHAT IN A HIGH-SCHOOL CLASSROOM (ABOVE), AND YOUNGER CHILDREN MAKE HANDICRAFTS IN A PRIMARY SCHOOL (BELOW).

LEARNING

15-m-high slanting bookcases refer to education in the big city, where 'the sky is the limit'. Facts and figures about education in the different cities are displayed on blackboards, so that the cities can easily be compared with each other in this pavilion, too. Films show the children from the six families going to school, sitting in class, making things with their hands, learning arithmetic, having music lessons or going to jazz ballet. ■

VISITORS LOOK UP, PAST TALL BOOKCASES AND LARGE VIDEO SCREENS, AT AN ARTIFICIAL CLOUD COVER 15 M OVERHEAD.

URBANIAN PAVILION

LOCATION World Expo 2010, Shanghai, China
DESIGN Kossmann.dejong (kossmanndejong.nl)
AREA 15,000 m^2
HEIGHT 22 m
CONTENT RESEARCH AND ADVISERS Arnold Reijndorp, Michelle Provoost, Paul Meurs
PROJECT MANAGEMENT Kossmann.dejong, Adelina Lee
MEDIA-CONTENT CONCEPT Kossmann.dejong, Tungsten Studio, De Aanpak
LIGHTING DESIGN Tweebeeke Licht
MEDIA-CONTENT PRODUCTION yU+co.[sh], Kossmann.dejong
ON-SCREEN GRAPHIC DESIGN yU+co.[lab], Kossmann.dejong
AUDIOVISUAL TECHNICAL CONSULTANTS yU+co.[lab]
CROWD-CONTROL CONSULTANTS Incontrol Simulation Solutions
CONTRACTOR Guangdong Jimei Design and Construction Company
LIGHTING AND AUDIO HARDWARE Shanghai Yong Jia Lighting and Audio Contracting
AUDIOVISUAL HARDWARE AND SHOW CONTROL Shanghai Foremost Multimedia
TECHNICAL AND PROJECT CONSULTANTS (DESIGN PHASE) Hypsos Leisure Asia
STARTED August 2007
COMPLETED May 2010

HEALTH

In the middle of the space, which is finished with white tiles, a round, half-transparent screen is suspended. Water runs down the walls and droplets fall from the leafy ceiling. The screen moves gently in the breeze created by the fans and the smell of eucalyptus fills the air. In de film projected on the inside of the screen, the six families can be seen going to the fitness club, the market and the butcher's. Images of babies are accompanied by displays of life expectancy data in the various cities. Other images show that the percentage of overweight people in São Paolo is many times less than in Melbourne and Rotterdam. ■■■■

DROPLETS FALL FROM A LEAFY CANOPY AT THE CENTRE
OF THE PAVILION.

THE BOOK BUILDING

SOU FUJIMOTO swims against the tide of digitization with his endless bookcases for the MUSASHINO ART UNIVERSITY LIBRARY AND MUSEUM.

WORDS **CATHELIJNE NUIJSINK**
PHOTOS **IWAN BAAN**

In many libraries, digitization is in full swing and more and more bookcases are disappearing to free up space. However, Sou Fujimoto's design for the Musashino Art University Museum & Library is an old-fashioned *bibliothèkè* that can be filled to the rafters with original volumes.

'The librarians had two significant requests,' Fujimoto told *Frame* in an interview back in 2007, shortly after winning the competition for the Musashino Art University Museum & Library. Bent over a gigantic scale model on the desk in the studio he occupied at the time in Nakano-Fujimicho, he explained the challenges of the design assignment. 'In the first place they wanted a space that functions as a searching system in itself. Secondly, they liked the idea of a library where you can feel as free as if you were wandering around in a forest.' Fujimoto solved

the two problems with a single clear concept. All he needed was a *gürü gürü*, a spiral form used in ancient times. By means of spiral geometry, he managed to use one simple gesture to erect a library that consists of a seemingly endless bookcase. 'A *gürü gürü* is a shape that can externalize the entire interior while at the same time it internalizes the exteriority,' continued Fujimoto. 'Its slight undulations create a variety of places; places to ponder, to linger, or to sit and simply immerse oneself in a story.'

The back-to-basics concept for the library is no exception in the Sou Fujimoto Office's portfolio. In practically all the designs he has created since he set up his own firm in 2000, there is a reference to ancient architectural forms such as caves or nests, or to the natural organization concealed behind the form of

a tree, for instance. Fujimoto points out that for him it is not about making an exact copy of a archetypical space the way we imagine it to look, but about the experience and the feeling the image of the form evokes in him. 'Instead of a modern library with only digital books, I prefer the pure origins of a library. The library I designed grows and grows, slowly turning into a bigger space.'

The endless bookcases in the library at the Musashino Art University seem to be trying to match the endlessness of the universe. Fujimoto drew his inspiration from the Argentinean poet and writer Jorge Luis Borges (1899-1986). Borges' imaginary Library of Babel makes the same depiction of infinity and tells with the same passion about the boundless possibilities it conjures up. 'Borges' Library of Babel is >>>

SOU FUJIMOTO'S BACK-TO-BASIC DESIGN FOR THE
MUSASHINO ART UNIVERSITY MUSEUM & LIBRARY
IS THAT OF AN OLD-FASHIONED BIBLIOTHÈKE.

BOOKCASES ARE ALSO PART OF THE FAÇADE, WHERE
THEY ARE SHIELDED BY GLASS PANES.

the ultimate library, containing all the literature you can imagine,' says Fujimoto. 'It's a library that has never existed and never will'.

More than three years after winning the competition, the library on the Tokyo campus has become reality. While strolling through the brand-new 'forest of books', Fujimoto explains how the space functions. The tour begins in the middle of the space, at the issuing counter. From this point, the books are divided into 'cake wedges' per category. 'Similar to a clock, you will find that each area is categorized in a radial manner,' Fujimoto relates while he indicates all the corners of the library. 'When one stands in front of the counter at the centre of the spiral, the different categories are visible. With this in mind, you can find the area of your choice by using only your instinct.' The layout of the various categories is both practical and instinctive. On the one hand, it allows systemic searching due to its well-thought out arrangement, but it's also possible to wander around as if in a forest without a clearly laid-out path. If you are not interested in systematic organization, you can allow yourself to be led by the curves of the walls of bookshelves until you stumble upon an interesting book by accident.

'Borges' Library of Babel is the ultimate library, containing all the literature you can imagine'
Sou Fujimoto

Browsing the library, it appears that the spatial experience is richer than the spiral-shaped floor plan would lead you to expect. The secret lies in the large square windows set into the walls of books. 'The punctured bookshelves, seen in a layered manner, give a sense of anticipation towards the space behind. The huge bookshelf walls guide people along the spiral into an invisible space.' Although you do not grasp the helix geometry in its entirety as you walk around the library, the form and the perspectives do make you unconsciously curious about the unknown spaces concealed behind what is visible. 'Most of the books are displayed on the shelves, in open stack, so books can be easily found, seen, picked up, and browsed through on the spot,' explains Fujimoto. 'It makes you want to stop, sit, and read.'

The idea of a woodland walk is intensified by the quality of the light. Daylight enters through openings shaped like cracks in the polycarbonate sheets in the ceiling, 'akin to light rays percolating through the canopy of fissures in clouds', according to Fujimoto. With his design, Fujimoto wants to make clear that only a collection of real books can induce a healthy dose of human curiosity. No digital collection can match this forest. 'You feel the presence of books in every spot in this library,' says Fujimoto at the end of the guided tour. 'Precisely this feeling of being surrounded by many, many books is very fundamental to me.' ▬▬

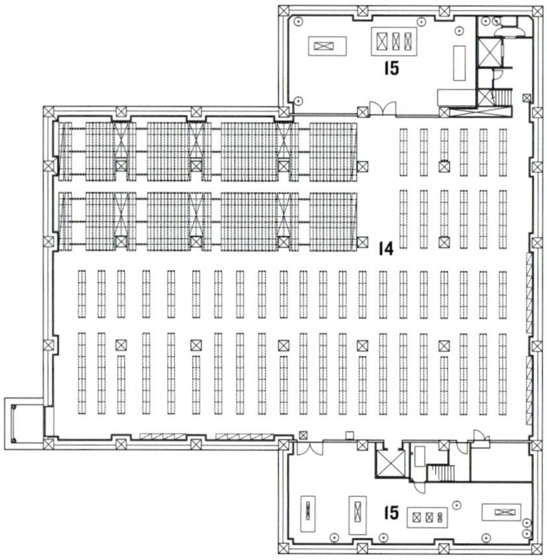

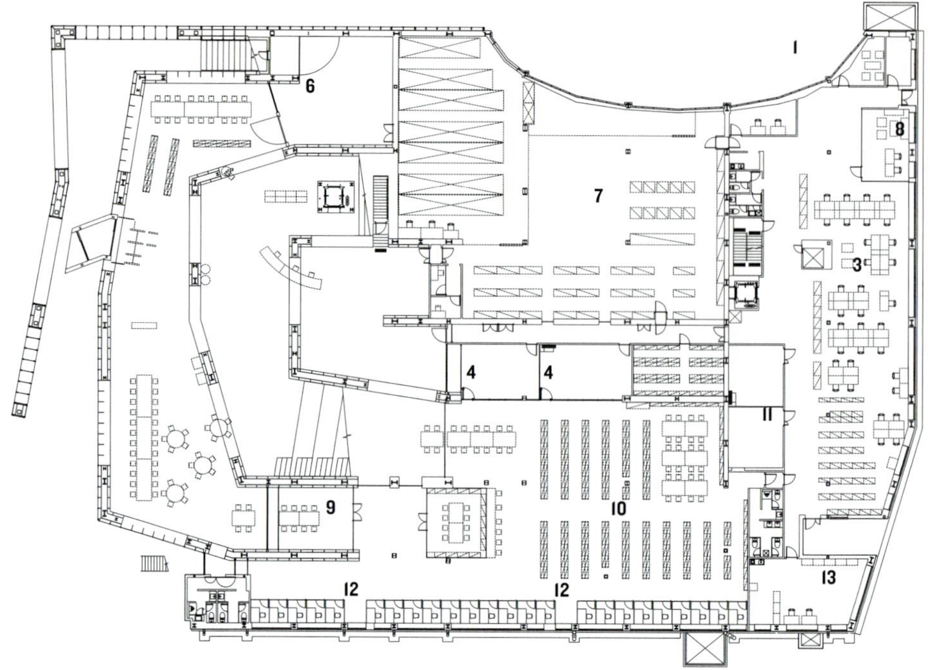

BASEMENT.

GROUND FLOOR.

1. ENTRANCE AREA
2. OPEN-STACK LIBRARY
3. OFFICES
4. READING ROOM
5. STUDENT READING ROOM
6. EXHIBITION SPACE
7. VALUABLE STACK
8. CHIEF LIBRARIAN'S ROOM
9. BOOK GALLERY
10. CATALOGUE GALLERY
11. MEETING ROOM
12. STUDY CUBICLES
13. LOUNGE
14. CLOSED STACK
15. MECHANICAL ROOM

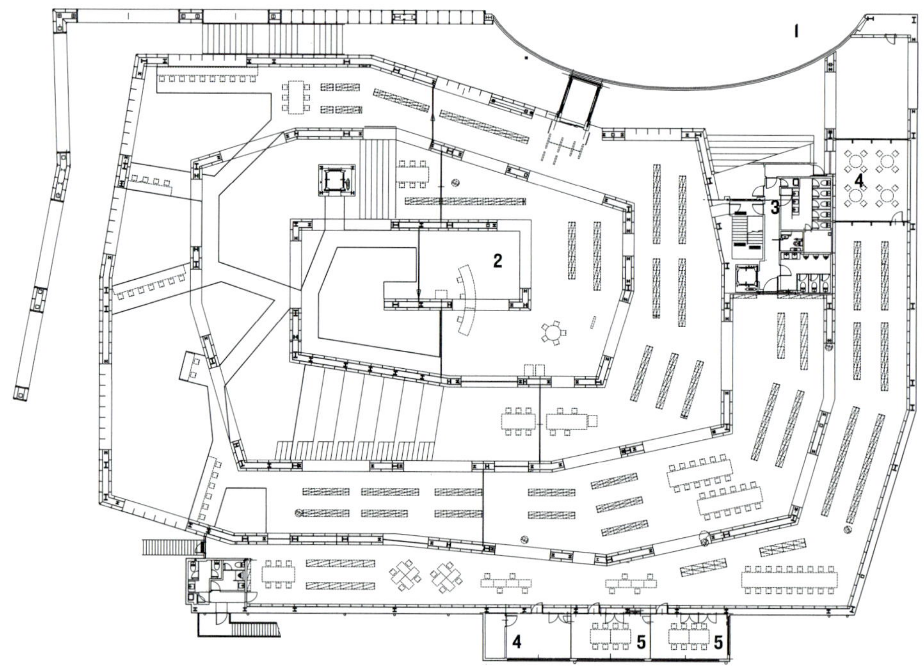

FIRST FLOOR (ABOVE MEZZANINE).

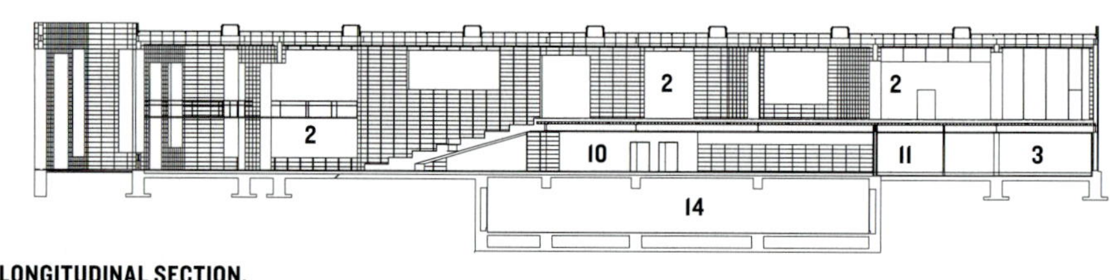

LONGITUDINAL SECTION.

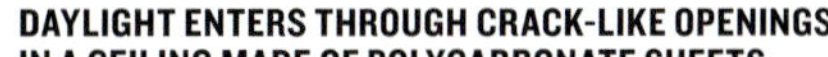

THE RHYTHM OF THE BOOKCASES CONTINUES IN THE
HIGH GLAZED 'GATEWAY WALL' OUTSIDE.

'Instead of a modern digitized library, I prefer the pure origins of a library'
Sou Fujimoto

DAYLIGHT ENTERS THROUGH CRACK-LIKE OPENINGS
IN A CEILING MADE OF POLYCARBONATE SHEETS.

MUSASHINO ART UNIVERSITY MUSEUM & LIBRARY

LOCATION 1-736 Ogawa-cho, Kodaira-shi,
Tokyo 187-8505, Japan
DESIGNER Sou Fujimoto Architects (sou-fujimoto.com)
CLIENT Musashino Art University
AREA 6,419.17 m²
FURNITURE Custom made: Inoue Industries; Ready-made:
03 Chair by Martin Van Severen, SIM by Jasper Morrison,
Chair by TENDO CO, Tom vac by Ron Arad
LIGHTING Spotlights: USHIOSPAX; Pendant lights: Maxray
COMPLETED March 2010

TO TEMPT VISITORS TO STOP, SIT AND READ, THE ARCHITECT
DESIGNED AN OPEN-STACK LIBRARY IN WHICH MOST
OF THE BOOKS ARE DISPLAYED ON SHELVES.

KAFFEE CALIFOI

FREELAND BUCK distils a modernist Viennese coffee-house vibe into an on-the-go eatery in Los Angeles.

WORDS **MICHAEL WEBB**
PHOTOS **LAWRENCE ANDERSON**

Los Angeles may be the world capital of fast food, with its proliferation of eateries selling everything from basic burgers and pizza to street snacks popular in Asia and Latin America. Earl's Gourmet Grub employs sophisticated design to stand out from the crowd and generate attention for its artisanal sandwiches and groceries. As the name suggests, it's a hybrid: basic fare made and served with care in a space that was shaped by computer technology and inspired by early expressions of modernism. Torqued light scoops and a frieze of plywood baffles articulate a linear space connecting the street to a rear patio. It's an elegant and sculpturally rich interior, created by fledgling architecture practice Freeland Buck. Though the two partners – David Freeland in LA and Brennan Buck in New York – have built little, Earl's is the product of intensive research and their fascination with digital fabrication and pattern making.

Buck explored ideas of layering and porosity in a temporary installation he developed with his students at the University of Applied Arts in Vienna during a teaching assignment he shared with Greg Lynn. They varied the size of openings so that colours would bleed from one layer to another. Freeland challenged his students to create a pattern that would unify disparate constructions and breach the boundaries of a black-walled gallery. Those explorations of form and pattern fed directly into Earl's. 'We wanted to take things we had been looking at in the context of a gallery and employ them as a welcoming environment for everyday activities,' says Buck.

Another source of inspiration was the modernist coffee house that Otto Wagner and his contemporaries created in Vienna a century ago. Linear spaces stripped of ornament and furnished with elegant bentwood chairs and pedestal tables, they marked a bold reaction against the claustrophobic décor of 19th-century interiors. Buck was impressed by the gleaming white vaulted ceilings and the monochromatic colour schemes. These early ventures into modernism have become hallowed monuments, where the Viennese still gather to chat and linger for hours over a coffee or newspaper. Nothing could be further removed culturally from America, where people settle for a Styrofoam cup of coffee and something to eat on the run. And yet, though Earl's is located on an urban highway and geared to the takeout trade, it is infused with the spirit of Vienna, subtly distilled. Three elements – a tiled façade, a wide >>>

ACCENTS OF BRIGHT RED ARE REVEALED WHEN THE
PLYWOOD BAFFLES ARE VIEWED FROM A CERTAIN ANGLE.

HIGH COUNTERS PROVIDE SPACE FOR
CUSTOMERS TO DINE ON THE GO.

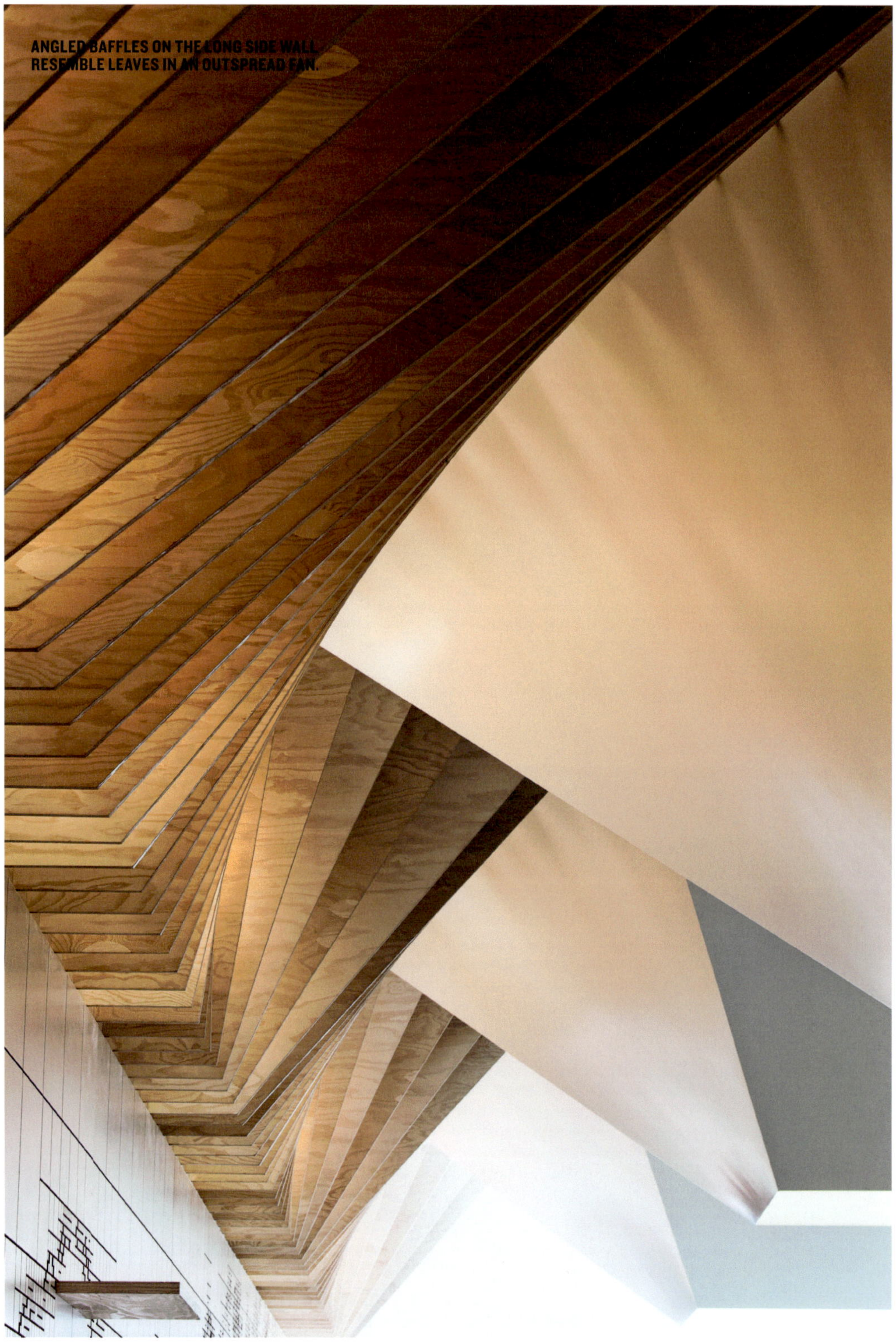

'We put everyday activities into a gallery context'
Brennan Buck

window that frames the interior, and a sign cut out of a plywood board and backlit at night – signal your arrival at a place that's out of the ordinary. Adolf Loos employed the same subtle understatement in the commercial block that is named for him across from the pompous Hofburg in Vienna. He had a larger site and budget with which to create his masterpiece; Freeland Buck was short on both and had to make inventive use of humbler materials. The designers decided to animate the linear space with three torqued light scoops: one frames a skylight and the other two are artificially lit.

Digital designs were mocked up at different scales, and the architects conducted experiments to see how far they could bend gypsum board and create curvilinear surfaces on the suspended frames. High-gloss white paint was applied to the scoops (as it was to the ceilings and walls of the Viennese cafés) to reflect as well as to channel the light over the white-marble serving counter. These two expanses of white bracket the prep kitchen and staff, and set off a row of loaves from which Earl's sandwiches are made to order.

On the long side wall, angled baffles of bleached plywood form a frieze that merges into the angled scoops at the midpoint of the store and continues on to the rear. They resemble leaves in an outspread fan as you approach, and seem to oscillate in the light of fluorescent strips set into a band of red on the rear wall. The colour spills through and is revealed as you view the baffles end on. Below this frieze is a mural that abstracts an image of the Alps. The pixellated relief was CNC-routed from maple-veneered MDF using Rhino and Grasshopper software. Display shelves of clear-coated plywood are set into the mural, with storage cabinets at the base of the wall. The design evolved over a period of six months, as the architects sought to organize the space productively and create an intangible atmosphere. In an earlier plan, chairs and tables occupy the front section, but these have been banished to the rear patio, leaving only a few high stools drawn up to a window counter. Customers carry off their sandwiches or stand at the counter to eat them. Though this solution was dictated by onerous health regulations, it aptly expresses the informality of LA and of a younger generation worldwide. The Viennese, innately conservative, will continue to cherish their old cafés, but Earl's may prove to be a model for the century to come. ■

HIGH-GLOSS WHITE PAINT WAS APPLIED TO THE SCOOPS TO REFLECT AS WELL AS TO CHANNEL THE LIGHT OVER THE WHITE-MARBLE SERVING COUNTER.

AN ABSTRACTED IMAGE OF THE ALPS WAS
CNC-ROUTED FROM MAPLE-VENEERED MDF.

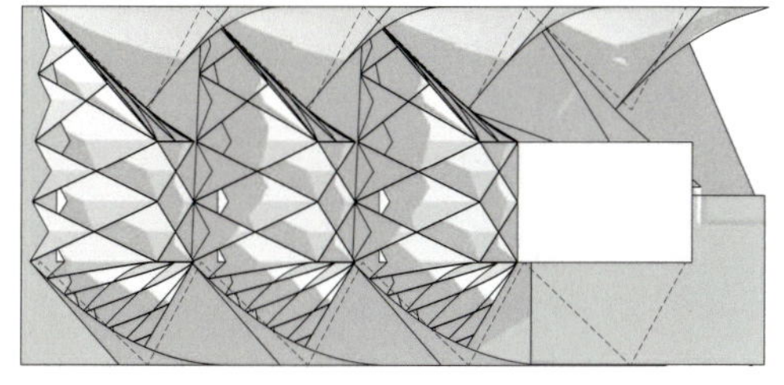
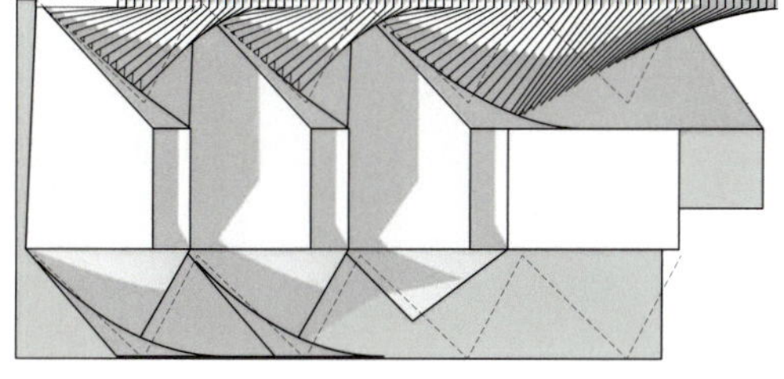
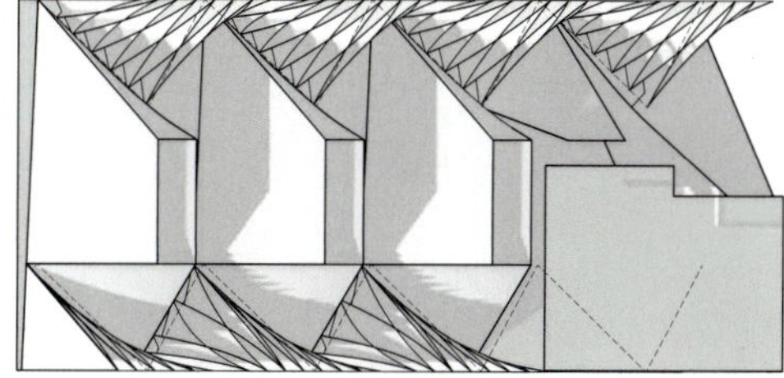
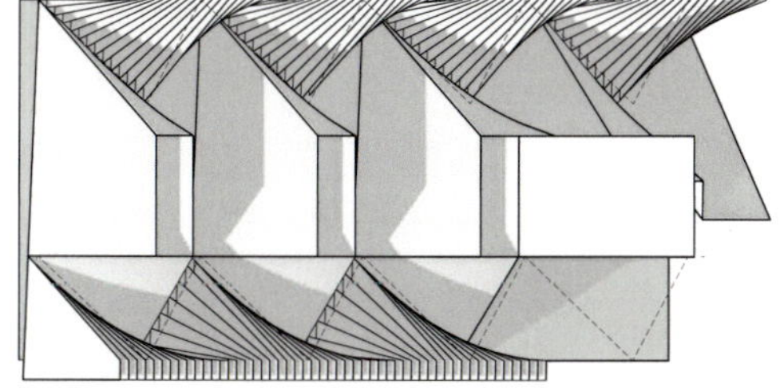
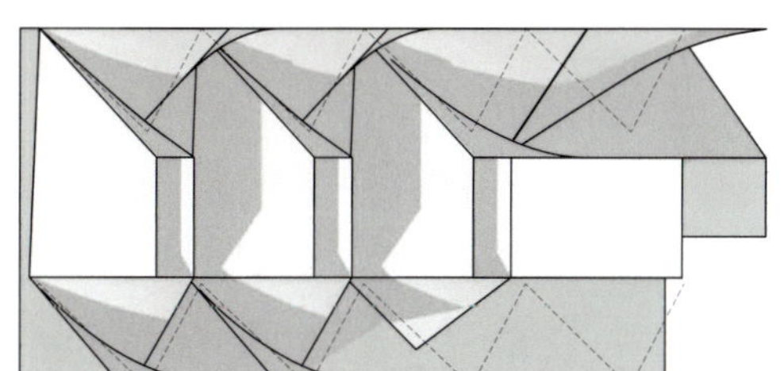

FREELAND BUCK EXPERIMENTED WITH DIFFERENT CEILING CONFIGURATIONS BEFORE SELECTING ANGLED BAFFLES FOR THE LONG SIDE WALL.

I. FRONT DOOR
2. SEATING / DISPLAY
3. MARBLE COUNTER
4. REGISTER
5. OPEN KITCHEN
6. BACK KITCHEN
7. TOILET
8. COOLER
9. SOFFIT

CEILING CONTOURS.

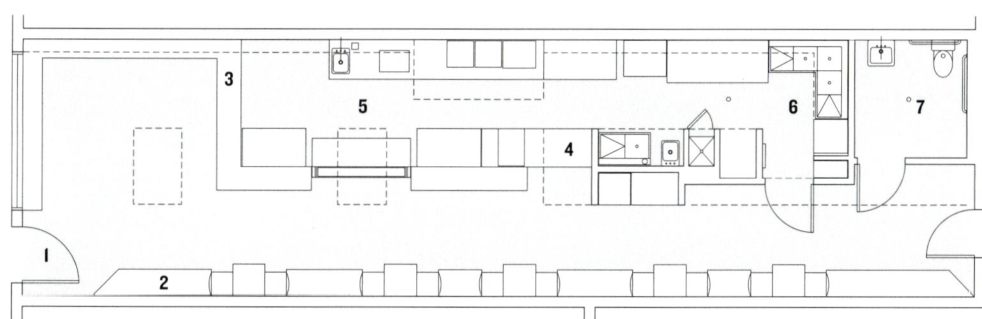

FLOOR PLAN.

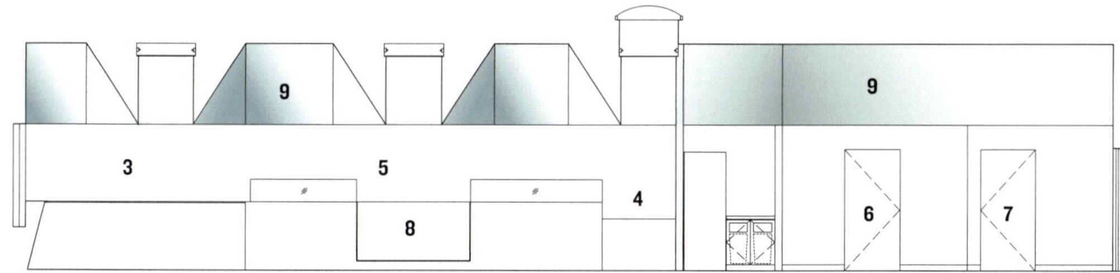

SECTION LOOKING EAST.

EARL'S GOURMET GRUB

LOCATION 12226 Venice Boulevard, Mar Vista CA 90066, Los Angeles, USA
DESIGNER Freeland Buck (freelandbuck.com)
CLIENT Earl's Gourmet Grub
AREA 150 m²
BUDGET €175,000
COMPLETED April 2010

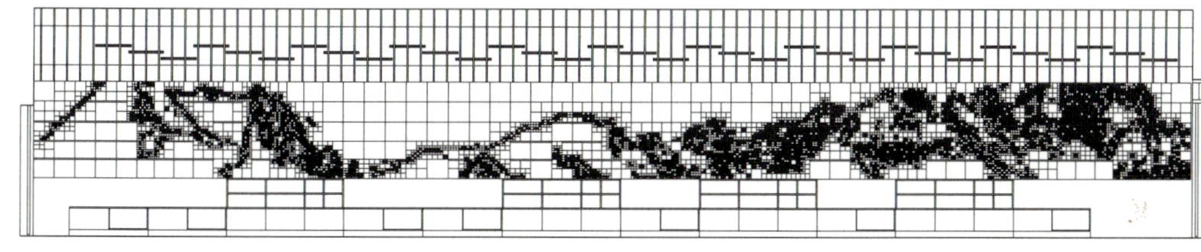

WEST ELEVATION.

REPORTS

DESIGN IN BUSINESS

SEE RONAN AND ERWAN BOUROULLEC'S TIMELESS BATHROOM
COLLECTION FOR AXOR ON PAGE 166.
PHOTO PAUL TAHON

CEO PAUL VAN DEN BERG SURROUNDED BY A BATCH OF NEWLY FORM-MOULDED SEATS FOR THE COMPANY'S LOTUS CHAIR.

FORM, FAMILY, FUNCTION

As paterfamilias and CEO, PAUL VAN DEN BERG puts together the MONTIS collection: a line of furniture based on craftsmanship and a love of materials.

WORDS **FEMKE DE WILD**
PHOTOS **DANIEL NICOLAS**

While Lobke van den Berg explains how she manages the Montis marketing department from her home in Barcelona, her father and company CEO Paul van den Berg makes a quick phone call. We're standing in the 'Montis Theatre' in the southern Netherlands, the showroom that hosts an annual presentation of the firm's latest furniture designs for important dealers before Montis takes its latest collection to the trade fair in Cologne. A quintessential family business, Montis was founded in 1974 by Paul's brothers, Ton and Gerard van den Berg. The furniture made here continues the family's dedication to quality and fine craftsmanship.

'In the beginning, we were real pioneers,' says Paul. 'We wanted to build a reputation based on furniture made exclusively of metal and leather, which was highly unusual at the time.'

While the three brothers worked on developing the product line, Paul often travelled abroad to sell their designs directly to stores, particularly those in the United States. In the 1970s, the design world was a small, closed circuit that was hard to penetrate, especially for a young Dutch company with little experience. 'When the oil crisis erupted in 1980, we grabbed our chance. People were looking for fresh solutions, and we managed to get our foot in the door. Suddenly we were meeting with Italian manufacturers and on our way to establishing a network of dealers. Dealers who satisfied our particular needs.'

At first, they kept their designs as simple as possible, but in the mid-1990s Montis started working with foam moulding, a production method that gradually became the company's speciality. 'We've always been a bit opportunistic,' says Paul. 'When presented with an opportunity, we seize it with both hands. After seeing how much freedom foam moulding was giving designers, we immediately installed the necessary equipment here at Montis. A mould is very expensive, but in terms of design technology, it's raised our operation to a completely different level. Since we've started using foam-moulding technology, our furniture has become much more suitable for the contract market. It's made our designs more refined; they have the appeal of consumer products but still reflect solid quality, and it's easier to turn out larger series. What's more, as a manufacturing method foam moulding benefits society.' Foam is very durable and thus produces a minimum of waste; it's easy to separate from the frame and just as easy to recycle. 'We limit the emission of

AT THE 'MONTIS THEATRE' SHOWROOM, THE COMPANY
PRESENTS THE FIRM'S LATEST FURNITURE DESIGNS TO
IMPORTANT DEALERS.

chemical substances by filtering the air we use before releasing it into the atmosphere outside the factory,' says Paul. 'Montis is deeply aware of the need for a cleaner environment.'

From the Montis Theatre, we enter the foam-moulding facility, an enormous space that houses a large number of moulds. A factory worker places a metal frame in the mould for the Ella chair and connects it to a machine that injects the correct polyurethane compound into the mould. Eight minutes later the seat of the chair has been completed. We walk a bit farther to a facility where, soft, comfortable layers of padding are glued to the wooden frames of pieces such as Axel, which for years has been Montis's bestselling sofa. In the next area we see Haşmet at a machine that scans pieces of leather for flaws and calculates the most

economical way to cut the panels needed for a certain model from a particular hide. 'We're constantly competing with the machine and ending up with fewer scraps,' says Hans, who's at the neighbouring table doing the same sort of work, but by hand. He learned the trade from a shoemaker and has been employed by Montis for 17 years. 'I work here because I love my job, which is a matter of putting puzzles together all day long,' he says. 'Not many companies are still cutting these pieces manually.' The few remnants that remain after cutting are used as samples or to make handicrafts in sheltered workshops and schools. Nothing is wasted.

Paul's father, who also ran a furniture company, sent his son to a school in this part of the country to study textiles. Soon after graduating, Paul took off for Germany and

Canada to gain commercial experience and to upgrade his language skills. 'Communication is a means of securing a good market position,' he says. 'And communicating is something I learned to do well during my time abroad.' His first love, however – for textiles and for materials in general – is clearly visible in the care that Montis takes when selecting and using leather. Stored in the cutting facility is an impressive supply of hides and skins in a wide range of types and colours. 'The quality of the materials used to cover the furniture determines at least 50 per cent of the quality of your product,' says Paul. 'The leather we use has to comply with our precise specifications.'

Montis's designs are modest, solidly constructed and characterized by fluid lines. 'Indeed, we do have a recognizable >>>

THE POLYURETHANE COMPOUND IS INJECTED INTO THE MOULD. WITHIN EIGHT MINUTES, THE SEAT OF THE CHAIR IS COMPLETED.

A METAL FRAME FOR ELLA – A CHAIR DESIGNED BY NIELS BENDTSEN – GOES INTO THE MOULD.

A MACHINE SCANS A PIECE OF LEATHER TO DETERMINE NOT ONLY ITS QUALITY BUT ALSO THE BEST (MOST ECONOMICAL) WAY TO USE IT IN MAKING A CHAIR.

EXCLUSIVE PIECES OF LEATHER ARE EVALUATED AND CUT BY AN EMPLOYEE WITH YEARS OF EXPERIENCE IN EXAMINING LEATHER. THE RESULT IS AN ABSOLUTE MINIMUM OF WASTE.

A FABRIC COVERING IS ADDED TO THE ELLA CHAIR.

IN THE SEWING DEPARTMENT, FURNITURE COVERINGS ARE STITCHED TOGETHER.

**PAUL VAN DEN BERG,
CEO OF MONTIS.**

MONTIS

WEBSITE montis.nl
LOCATION Steenstraat 2, 5107 NE Dongen, the Netherlands
ESTABLISHED 1974
AREA OF DISTRIBUTION Worldwide
MARKET SECTOR Consumer and contract furniture
BESTSELLING PRODUCTS Axel, Windy, Impala, Lotus, Loge, Turner.
COLLABORATING DESIGNERS Gerard van den Berg, Niels Bendtsen, Christophe Marchand, Dick Spierenburg, Gijs Papavoine, Simon Pengelly, Bertjan Pot and more

'Our designs have to be functional; we don't want to become elitist'
Paul van den Berg

ELLA IS AVAILABLE WITH A STRIP-STEEL SLED BASE OR A FOUR-LEGGED SWIVEL BASE. THE CHAIR IS SUITABLE FOR BOTH THE CONSUMER AND THE CONTRACT MARKETS.

style,' says Paul. 'Our designs have a sense of movement, what you might call *Schwung*.' Paul himself selects designs for the collection. He and Gijs Papavoine, who replaced Gerard van den Berg in 1990 as head designer, go looking for new designers, a process that involves considering what's missing in the collection. Several years ago the company introduced the Montis+ collection, a platform for young designers. 'There's a huge gap – a sort of purgatory – between design talent and the manufacturer with a strictly industrial mind-set. We adopt experimental designs and examine the feasibility of their manufacture.' The Lazy Bastard, designed by Bertjan Pot, is a successful example; it's been a good seller, but Montis is less interested in the commercial value of the collection. 'Retailers want products that are

popular with shoppers, but the press wants to see experiments. Montis+ is a medium. We're inventive and experimental, but our designs have to be functional. We don't want to become elitist.'

Furniture made by Montis is part of a sector that's been hit hard by the economic crisis. With governmental support (unemployment benefits), the company has been able to maintain its full staff and their invaluable know-how; no one had to be let go. 'We're in the recovery phase now,' says Paul. 'The contract market was the first to collapse, but it's also been the first to pick up again. Contract projects are responsible for only 30 per cent of our turnover; the other 70 per cent of our business comes from the residential market. And governmental projects didn't slow down during the slump – town halls, schools and

hospitals, for example. We're seeing a major change in the health-care sector,' he continues. 'There's more diversification. Rather than very plain furniture, these facilities want pieces that complement a residential atmosphere.'

From the pioneering phase in the early years, Montis has evolved into a company that's placing more and more importance on industrialization, automatization and policy development. 'In the beginning, it was really a matter of one for all and all for one. Although that changes to a degree as you grow, ultimately the idea behind the way we work has remained the same,' says Paul. 'I'm a generalist, a guy who knows a little bit about everything and who's mainly interested in gathering together all aspects involved in this work. The whole – the sum total of all the parts – that's what it's all about.' ■

OF THE FIRST WATER

CEO PHILIPPE GROHE asked the BOUROULLECS to create a new bathroom collection for AXOR, 'because these designers consciously influence space'.

WORDS **CHRIS SCOTT**
PHOTOS **PAUL TAHON, COURTESY OF RONAN AND ERWAN BOUROULLEC**

Hansgrohe, global leader in bathroom and shower fittings, is moving even further into the world of innovative style with its design brand, Axor. Klaus Grohe – son of founder and namesake Hans Grohe, who established the company in Schiltach, Germany, in 1901 – began working with designers 40 years ago. Today his son Philippe, who heads Axor, continues to do so. Philippe Grohe's most recent collaboration was with French designers Ronan and Erwan Bouroullec, creators of the Axor/Bouroullec bathroom collection, a line of products that offers a raft of new possibilities. The quality of these items, says Philippe Grohe, comes along 'once every 20 years if you're lucky'.

Can you tell us about the designers involved in the Axor collection?
Philippe Grohe: Axor has no in-house designers,

because we want to avoid the closeness that leads to repetition or monotony – and to rule out conflicts with outside designers. But we do have an excellent and experienced group of employees that others might see as a design team. With their background and open-minded approach, they form an intrinsic part of the design process, working with external designers to find solutions, providing them with the expertise of a global company – and that includes the power of innovation, a solid distribution network and a culture of understanding. Choosing the designers we work with is my responsibility. It's the most important decision I take.

What are your criteria?
It's crucial to have a positive rapport with the designers I select. After all, we will be working together for years. I look for designers

who've got something to say, designers with a philosophy. It's about more than a portfolio of projects from which to choose. These people are often more than just product designers. Sometimes we work with architects or interior designers. At the end of the 1990s, I formulated a strategy. I wanted to work with people who understand and work with space and who focus on solutions. These are things the Bouroullecs do so well. They consciously influence space.
How strict is the briefing your designers get?
It would be crazy to give a formal briefing. I talk with them, listen to as many of their insights as possible, and tap into what I hear. We engage in a wide-open discussion that includes an intense exchange of ideas – not just about products but about how to live in this bathroom they're designing. >>>

SMOOTH, SIMPLE SHAPES CHARACTERIZE THE SHOWER UNITS,
AS WELL AS THE REST OF THE COLLECTION.

AXOR/BOUROULLEC BATHROOM COLLECTION

The Axor/Bouroullec bathroom collection was a learning process for all involved. The project took six years, and the result is a pure, simple and timeless line of products. Brothers Ronan and Erwan Bouroullec were delighted to work on a complete collection, as opposed to individual pieces; to consider the ergonomics of the space; and to search for a subtle 'white language' of harmony, sensuality, softness and elegance – all in relation to the human body. No superfluous details, but smooth, simple shapes. No sharp corners, but surfaces inviting to the touch. In the words of the Bouroullecs: 'Early in the morning, after a late night, you do not particularly want to be faced with a conceptual project. You just want something that works well.' The collection – comprising 85 elements and highlighted by a washbasin – invites the user to create a personalized bathroom based on an endless number of possibilities. No longer do mixers or controls have to be placed in certain positions. After Axor/Bouroullec products leave the store, they begin to lead their own exciting lives.

'I want to work with people who understand space and concentrate on solutions'
Philippe Grohe

LINE SKETCHES CONVEY THE SIMPLE SHAPES THAT EPITOMIZE THE BOUROULLECS' PROJECT.

THE FORMULATION OF A COLLECTION RATHER THAN A
SERIES OF INDIVIDUAL PIECES ADHERES TO AXOR'S HOLISTIC
APPROACH TO DESIGN.

PHILIPPE GROHE,
CEO OF AXOR.

AXOR

WEBSITES hansgrohe.com, axor-design.com
LOCATION Hansgrohe AG, Auestrasse 5-9,
77761 Schiltach, Germany
ESTABLISHED Hansgrohe in 1901, Axor in 1994
AREA OF DISTRIBUTION Worldwide
MARKET SECTOR Sanitaryware
BESTSELLING PRODUCTS Axor Starck, Axor Citterio
COLLABORATING DESIGNERS Philippe Starck, Antonio
Citterio, Jean-Marie Massaud, Patricia Urquiola, Phoenix
Design, Ronan and Erwan Bouroullec

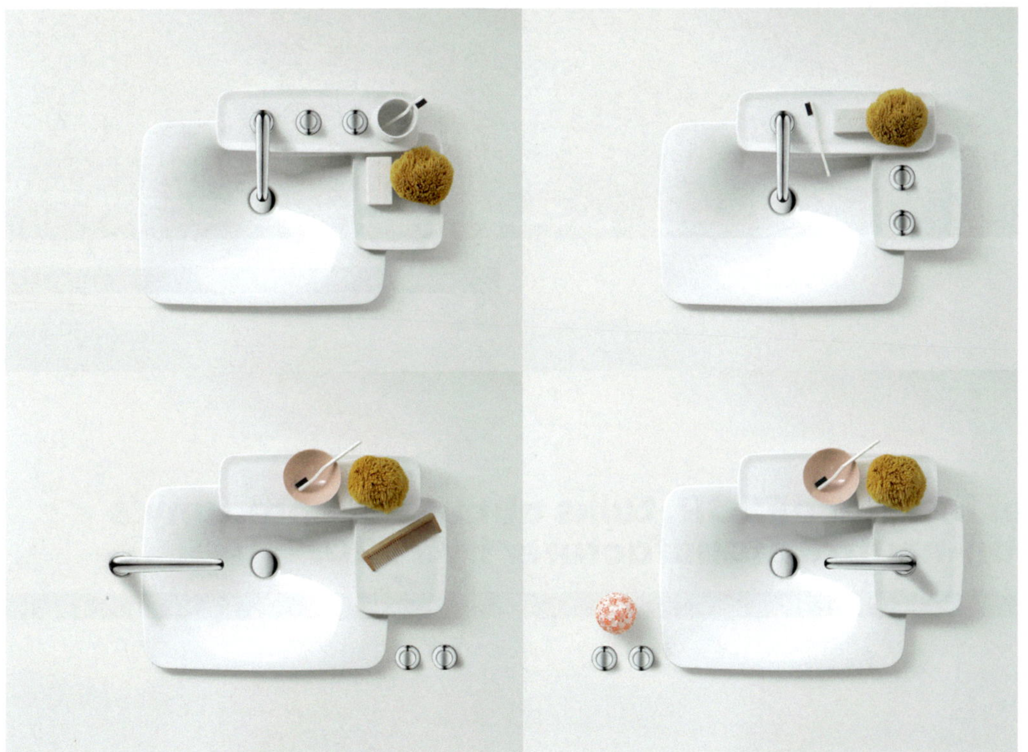

'The biggest challenge is water; people are using more and more of it'
Philippe Grohe

Can you describe the Axor approach?
We're an ecologically minded company that has green blood flowing in its veins. We take a holistic, visionary approach to design. I would like Axor to live the philosophy of architecture and of exploring solutions rather than simply proposing additional products. Here at Axor, design is the driving technology – a technology that needs to be reinvented time and again. We're constantly considering the direction that bathrooms will be taking in the future. Beyond its functional significance, the bathroom is increasingly a place of peace and relaxation, a retreat from life's fast pace.

What are the most important changes?
There is a huge difference between now and ten years ago. Architecture is moving into bathrooms, spaces are changing, and bathrooms are gaining importance as living areas. Such changes are picking up speed as we speak, but this is still a very conservative part of the home. About 80 per cent of today's bathrooms resemble those of yesterday. There are better things to do with space – like opening it up – and every one of our collections provides users with new and improved features. It's also important to have a structural, holistic approach. If one company makes mixers and another makes basins, nothing can change.

Have you just described your biggest challenge?
Our biggest challenge has to be water. People want and need a greater sense of wellbeing, which means that they use more water. It's not possible to continue like this; we have to find a solution. People often ask me how I can come up with yet another good idea. I have hundreds of ideas. They're lying all over the floor, so to speak. All you have to do is pick them up. Ideas are not a problem. The only problems are time and capacity. ■

FLOOR PLANS

LINDSEY PARNELL, CEO of InterfaceFLOR, talks about the company's mission to become a carbon-neutral manufacturer by 2020.

WORDS **CASSANDRA PIZZEY**
PHOTOS **COURTESY OF INTERFACEFLOR**

What is the history of InterfaceFLOR?
It all began with Ray Anderson in 1973. Soon after seeing his first carpet tile at Heuga during a visit to the Netherlands [Heuga was a flooring manufacturer now owned by InterfaceFLOR], Anderson introduced it in the US. Luckily, with the huge influx of IT companies in the 1980s, floor tiles became known as an ideal product for corporate offices that required easy installation and reparation of underfloor cabling.

Why select carpet tiles rather than regular carpeting? What's the difference?
Let's start with the production process: a conventional carpet is basically tufted yarn, whereas the standard 50-x-50-cm carpet tile has a backing material. Carpet tiles generate a lot less waste when laid. Because of the square format, it's easy to calculate how many tiles you need, and leftovers can be used elsewhere. You can't use remnants from normal carpeting in other spots, however, because of possible colour differences.

Have you seen many major changes over the years?
Since the mid-1990s, InterfaceFLOR has been developing a vision for the future. We want to become a sustainable manufacturer of carpet tiles. Because our manufacturing process requires various chemicals, we feel it's our duty to be as environmentally friendly as we can on all other fronts.

With factories on four continents, how do you achieve a high standard across the board?
Operating factories in Asia, North America, Europe and Australia demands a central monitoring system. We also use something called LCA (life cycle analysis) to compare the sustainability of our products. One criterion is the carbon footprint of a tile, from raw material to recycled product. If any part of the process were to generate higher-than-average carbon emissions, we would know about it.

InterfaceFLOR promotes itself as eco-friendly. Don't all companies have to be green nowadays?
Yes, certainly, but there's a big difference between designing products that can be recycled and actually using recycled materials. We have over 15 years of experience on our side, and we put it to good use. At InterfaceFLOR, sustainability is integrated into every part of the company, from production to shipping, and we aim to get our engineers and designers on board as well. >>>

TRIBAL RHYTHMS, PICTURED HERE, IS A RANGE OF PATTERNED TILES THAT CAN BE COMBINED TO CREATE AN ENDLESS ARRAY OF NEW LOOKS.

FRAGMENTS OF OLD CARPETS ARE RECYCLED AND REUSED IN THE PRODUCTION OF NEW CARPET TILES.

'It's our duty to be as environmentally friendly as we can'
Lindsey Parnell

EASTERN DELIGHTS (LEFT) IS INSPIRED BY THE OPULENCE OF THE MIDDLE EAST WHEREAS THE ORIENT (RIGHT) EMBODIES THE SUBTLETY FOUND IN EMBROIDERED KIMONOS.

ABOVE LEFT: USED CARPETS AND CARPET TILES ARE RETURNED TO THE INTERFACEFLOR FACTORY. ABOVE RIGHT: THE BACKING IS SEPARATED FROM THE TOP LAYER READY TO BE REUSED.

NYLON YARN, THE BIGGEST POLLUTER IN THE PROCESS, IS ALSO RECYCLED.

THE RESULTING FIBRES ARE RECYCLED TO MAKE NEW CARPET TILES.

GEARING THE MODE OF TRANSPORT TO SPECIFIC REGIONS REDUCES CARBON EMISSIONS. IN THE NETHERLANDS, TILES ARE TRANSPORTED BY BOAT.

LINDSEY PARNELL,
CEO OF INTERFACEFLOR.

INTERFACEFLOR

WEBSITE interfaceflor.eu
LOCATION Scherpenzeel (NL), Halifax (UK), Craigavon (I)
ESTABLISHED 1973
AREA OF DISTRIBUTION Worldwide
MARKET SECTOR Modular flooring
BESTSELLING PRODUCTS Heuga 726, Equilibrium, Transformation, Straightforward
ANNUAL TURNOVER (2009) €670,509,078

'We put our 15 years of experience in sustainability to good use'
Lindsey Parnell

ON SAFARI IS INSPIRED BY THE BOLD PATTERNS OF AFRICAN MUD CLOTH.

Can you explain how you plan to achieve your goal?
Recently, for instance, we introduced a high-precision sonic cutting machine. Not only does it cut more cleanly than a traditional stamp machine; even more importantly, it saves drastically on waste material, which would otherwise get thrown away. From a design aspect, we have a tile called Flat Weave, which uses only 50 per cent of the yarn needed to make a traditional tile. It features a much lower pile, which allows for a sharp tile design.

Why not manufacture only this type of floor tile?
We used to sell mainly to corporate offices, but currently we supply sectors such as hospitality, health care, education and government. Different needs call for different approaches. This autumn we introduced the Razzle Dazzle collection in Europe – tiles inspired by bright explosions such as fireworks and lightning. Razzle Dazzle is made from post-industrial recycled yarn. For that matter, certain lines manufactured in the US have been made from post-consumer recycled yarn for some time now.

What is post-consumer recycled yarn?
When a company decides to get new flooring, the old carpet tiles are returned to the factory, where the yarn and backing are separated and both components reworked into new tiles.

With all this recycling going on, is there still room for designing?
Not only do we pride ourselves on being the number-one leader in sales and sustainability; we also try to push the envelope on the design front. We release up to 20 new collections every year. We're very proud of our new World Textiles Collection, a selection of patterned floor tiles inspired by ethnic cultures from around the world. This range should make our customers say, 'Wow, I've never seen anything like this before.' The same element of surprise is reflected in our new ad campaign for the line.

What does the future hold for InterfaceFLOR?
InterfaceFLOR's biggest goal is to uphold the promise to eliminate any negative impact on the environment by 2020. We call it Mission Zero. ∎

FLEXFORM

CHAIRS AND SOFAS

▶ SEDIA 1
BY ENZO MARI
FOR ARTEK

A part of Enzo Mari's Autoprogettazione series for Artek, Sedia 1 consists of a set of pre-cut pine boards, some 50 nails and a set of instructions. The chair is accompanied by a documentary in which Mari explains the concept behind the chair.

artek.fi

▶ PLC
BY PEARSONLLOYD
FOR MODUS

A modern take on the classic café chair with separate seat and backrest, PLC comes with or without armrests in a multitude of satin-painted finishes. Padded cushions or upholstery in Harris Tweed is optional.

modusfurniture.co.uk

◀ SPRING
BY CUNO FROMMHERZ
FOR LEOLUX

The straight lines and feather-light frame of the Spring dining chair make it practical and easy on the eye. An integrated hand grip at the back of the chair ensures easy mobility. Available in three models, with and without armrests, in wood and with upholstered sides.

leolux.com

◀ LYNX
BY EWALT KOMMER, LAURENS SNEUJINK, AND JEROEN KORS
FOR CASALA

Lynx is a versatile chair suitable for quick transformations in spaces such as conference halls, hotels and waiting rooms. The chair has a hidden linkage system (patented) that allows for numerous possibilities. Available in three shells, various colours, and a number of materials and fabrics.

casala.com

◀ TRE 3
BY ANGELO MANGIAROTTI
FOR AGAPE CASA

A stool with a backrest? Although it has only three legs, Tre 3 is as stable as a normal four-legged chair, thanks to its solid T-shaped wooden base. A piece of leather seamlessly forms the seat and back of the chair.

agapecasa.it

▲ ZIPFRED
BY VIKTOR MATIC
FOR NILS HOLGER MOORMANN

Six pieces of ash wood, 20 layers of white corrugated cardboard and a handful of cable ties are all you need to make a Zipfred at home, in your living room or workshop. The DIY approach is reflected in the individual character of each perky Zipfred chair.

moormann.de

▲ TEAM
BY LIEVORE ALTHERR MOLINA
FOR ARPER

Responding to the functional needs of spaces designed for rapid and frequent changes, Team is a good choice for conference halls, auditoriums and offices. Arper's modular seating system is available in polypropylene or upholstered in a wide range of colours. With or without arms, the chair has various base options including four legs, sled and cantilever.

arper.com

▲ WOTU
BY DANTE BONUCCELLI
FOR LAMM

Following the principle of 'Use More Use Less', Dante Bonuccelli made the Wotu chair from layers of beech, avoiding the use of materials known to be harmful to nature. Wotu's elegant simplicity complements its durable, functional design.

lamm.it

▲ PETITE GIGUE
BY FRANÇOIS AZAMBOURG
FOR MOUSTACHE

Manufactured according to a marine-based technique (*à bouchain vif*), Petite Gigue is a surprisingly stable three-legged chair. The designer claims that the chair's stability is reinforced by the user, making it in fact a five-legged chair.

moustache.fr

▶ UPHOLSTERED TAPAS CHAIR
BY MATTHEW HILTON
FOR DE LA ESPADA

With a nod at Spanish design, this comfortable high-back dining chair boasts slimline upholstery and a unique three-legged shape – features that make for a compact piece of furniture. Comes in American black walnut or American white oak, and in a wide range of fabrics.

delaespada.com

▼ ANTELOPE
BY MONICA FÖRSTER
FOR SWEDESE

Antelope is made of solid ash. The seat, which comes with a fabric or leather covering, is upholstered in high-resilient foam. A matching table is available.

swedese.se

▼ HOMERUN
BY SYLVAIN WILLENZ
FOR KARIMOKU

Inspired by cartoon classics, Sylvain Willenz toned down the comedy to give his Homerun chair an elegant appeal. The wide seat and tapered legs do convey a naive charm, however, as do the available colours: yellow, charcoal, red and white.

karimoku-newstandard.jp

▲ 111 NAVY CHAIR
BY EMECO AND THE COCA-COLA
COMPANY

Based on the classic aluminium chair designed for the U.S. Navy in 1944, the aptly named 111 Navy chair incorporates approximately 111 recycled plastic bottles and is reinforced with glass fibre. Choose from six colours, including Coca-Cola Red, Snow and Charcoal.

emeco.net

▲ ABARTH CHAIR
BY FABIO NOVEMBRE
FOR CASAMANIA

Casamania, Fabio Novembre and Vivi combined forces to produce a chair driven by the Abarth brand – the auto-sport division of the Fiat Group. The choice of materials – polycarbonate and aluminium – and the chair's transparent 'windswept' profile evoke the world of car racing.

casamania.it

fatboy®

The Netherlands

Beyer Interieur
Harderwijk
www.beyer-interieur.nl

Paagman Den Haag
Den Haag
www.paagman.nl

Pretty 4U
Etten-Leur
www.pretty4u.nl

Ramon Future Furniture
Tilburg
www.ramonff.nl

Mister Design
Helmond
www.misterdesign.nl

Droomvisie Beddenspecialist
Wassenaar
www.droomvisie.nl

Eijerkamp
Veenendaal
www.eijerkamp.nl

Eijerkamp
Zutphen
www.eijerkamp.nl

Germany

Elimination
Waltersberg
www.elimination.de

Güterbahnhof 12 GmbH
Marburg
www.gueterbahnhof12.de

France

Hom'kara Vannes / SARL La Deco
du Golfe
Theix Vannes
02 97 42 40 73

limited edition dealer · limited edition dealer · limited edition dealer ·

fatboy

www.fatboy.com

▼ ZOE
BY FRANCO POLI
FOR MATTEO GRASSI

Zoe is the result of the ten years that Franco Poli has spent working with coach-hide mesh. The tubular-steel frame is covered in coach hide (Matteo Grassi's cutting technique is patented). The seat is padded in polyurethane foam. Finish in chrome or epoxy paint.

matteograssi.it

▼ DALLAS
BY VICENTE SOTO
FOR CAPDELL

With its minimalist Nordic look, metal frame, and beech seat and backrest, Dallas pays tribute to nature by incorporating wood from sustainable forests. Suitable for both the consumer and contract markets, the design is also available as a stool in two heights.

capdell.com

◄ CHAIR IV
BY TJ O'KEEFE

Best suited for the dining room, Chair IV is made of matte-painted solid wood with high-gloss interior panels. Owing to its precise angles and disguised construction, the chair looks very much like a 'live' computer-generated image. Available in black on black, red on red, and black on white.

tjokeefe.com

▼ YY CHAIR
BY FOR USE/NUMEN
FOR MOROSO

Diagonal wooden posts used to create the armrests of this chair not only improve stability but also merge into the legs to form two letters – a Y is clearly visible on each side of the chair. YY is made from solid beech or oak, varnished or oiled. The seat has an upholstered cushion.

moroso.it

▼ FAMILY CHAIR
BY JUNYA ISHIGAMI
FOR LIVING DIVANI

A number of differently shaped chairs comprise the remarkable Family collection. Thanks to a tubular-steel frame combined with a mesh backrest and seat, these chairs look virtually weightless. Finished with epoxy paint, the chair is available in many colours. The series includes an outdoor version.

livingdivani.it

► BRANCA
BY SAM HECHT
FOR MATTIAZZI

The branches of a tree provided inspiration for Branca, which melds innovative design and traditional materials. The jointless frame is made from one piece of solid wood with the aid of CNC technology. The chair comes in beech or ash and in a variety of seat and frame combinations.

mattiazzi.eu

▲ WOGG 50
BY JÖRG BONER
FOR WOGG

Taking advantage of developments in moulded-plywood technology, which rely on CNC milling, Jörg Boner came up with the light, stackable and multifunctional Wogg 50. The folded sides of the seat hold the legs and back in place. Colours are natural ash and black ash.

wogg.ch

▶ JOKO
BY BARTOLI DESIGN
FOR KRISTALIA

Joko has a cheerful, friendly look based on a simple, refined form and slightly angled backrest. Suitable for both consumer and contract markets, the metal-framed chair is upholstered in polyurethane foam and covered entirely in either fabric or leather (natural or synthetic).

kristalia.it

▶ NEVE
BY PIERO LISSONI
FOR PORRO

With its 1950s' style and soft yet vigorous lines, Neve reinterprets the classic wooden chair in a contemporary vein. The chair is available with or without arms in a choice of four colours: black-stained ash, red-stained ash, mongoi-stained ash and natural ash.

porro.com

▲ 5 O'CLOCK CHAIR
BY NIKA ZUPANC
FOR MOOOI

With a trace of pink roses like those on English bone-china tea sets, the 5 O'Clock Chair evokes a long-forgotten sense of romance. Blending tradition and innovation, the chair is made from black-stained beech and imitation leather. Choose from 24 prints.

moooi.com

◀ COMBACK CHAIR
BY PATRICIA URQUIOLA
FOR KARTELL

Adding a new chapter to English tradition, Patricia Urquiola has designed an updated version of the 18th-century Windsor chair. Urquiola's version embodies functionality and ergonomics while conveying a sense of lightness through the use of a thermoplastic technopolymer. Available in nine colours.

kartell.it

▶ NEST
BY ALEXANDER LERVIK
FOR JOHANSON DESIGN

Nest is a stable, comfy chair distinguished by the metal connectors that attach the legs to the seat. The Nest family includes a chair, a lounger, a table and a bar stool, all of which come in a variety of colours.

johansondesign.se

▲ FLUX
BY JERSZY SEYMOUR
FOR MAGIS

Representing a drawing floating in midair, Flux is a sturdy wire chair based on a flexible manufacturing technique. Jerszy Seymour treated each bent-wire element as an axis with unlimited directions, creating flowing lines that contrast with the chair's structured, modernist style.

magisdesign.com

▲ ORA-GAMI
BY ORA-ÏTO
FOR STEINER

The icon of the Ora-Gami collection, this polyurethane armchair consists of a single folded sheet of material. The frame – in black or white – is lined in the customer's choice of various Kvadrat fabrics.

steiner-paris.com

▼ LA CLASICA
BY JESÚS GASCA
FOR STUA

This stackable wooden chair translates all the principles of traditional chairs into a contemporary design. Curved to support the human body, La Clásica has a seat and backrest that fuse with its legs to create a fluid form. The seat is strengthened with a polypropylene insert.

stua.com

▶ DARLING
BY NIGEL COATES
FOR FRAG

Darling is an addition to Frag's 2008 Cara collection. In this case, variety is in the choice of bases: a total of five options. Shown here is a model with wooden legs. The seat is covered in soft leather.

frag.it

◀ ARHUS
BY SATELLIET

This down-to-earth chair captures the pure essence of nature with its solid-wood frame and seat. Reminiscent of the past, Arhus has an intriguing design that mixes straight and curvy lines. The chair is available in a variety of stains; also comes with a painted seat.

satelliet.net

▲ 130 SERIES
BY NAOTO FUKASAWA
FOR THONET

Part of the 130/1130 series of tables and chairs, the solid-wood dining chair pictured here has an ergonomically formed seat and backrest for optimum comfort. Select a model in plain wood with a padded seat, or choose a model with a completely upholstered seat and backrest. Finishes include natural or stained beech or oak.

thonet.eu

◀ SKETCH
BY BURKHARD VOGTHERR AND JONATHAN PRESTWICH FOR ARCO

An update of the classic bucket seat, Sketch is suitable for a variety of functions: it makes an elegant dining chair yet looks equally at home in the office. Clean lines and an understated style link the new model with the existing Arco range, while the circular upholstered seat – available in fabric, leather or a combination of the two – sets Sketch apart from its comrades.

arco.nl

▲ JRA2
BY JENNI ROININEN
FOR NIKARI

This simple yet stylish armchair unites wood and textile within a subtle play of lines. The collection includes chairs with and without armrests, a sofa, and complementary tables. JRA2 is available in ash, birch and oak. Chairs have removable padding.

nikari.fi

▲ BETTY
BY ANTONIO CITTERIO
FOR FLEXFORM

A solid-wood frame supports a seat made from the same material. Upholstered in polyurethane foam, the seat wears a protective fabric cover. Betty is also available with a leather-clad seat.

flexform.it

A totally captivating online destination for those who are searching for inspiration and unique coverage of modern design and trends

www.yatzer.com

▼ NAP
BY KASPER SALTO
FOR FRITZ HANSEN

Designed to accommodate three key sitting positions – described as 'normal', 'active' and 'passive' – NAP is a lightweight, stackable chair suitable for public, private and professional spaces. The curvaceous beauty is available in Milk White, Butter Yellow, Pepper Grey and Coffee Brown.

fritzhansen.com

▼ BELLOWS
BY TOAN NGUYEN
FOR WALTER KNOLL

Adopting the form of a flower stretching towards the sun, Bellows has a conical body that rises from a solid base before opening to form the seat. A smooth inner surface contrasts with soft folds on the exterior. The seat can be adjusted in height by up to 10 cm.

walterknoll.de

◄ EGO ROCK
BY PAPATYA

The stackable Ego Rock combines a polypropylene base with a polycarbonate back. Colours can be mixed and matched for a unique personal look. Thanks to anti-UV stabilization, the chair is also suitable for outdoor use.

papatya.com.tr

▼ NARA
BY SHIN AZUMI
FOR FREDERICIA

Playing homage to Scandinavian design while expressing the sculptural beauty of solid timber, Nara is a comfortable dining chair and a simple wooden object. The chair comes in oak or in solid ash finished in clear or black lacquer. Available with leather or fabric upholstery.

fredericia.com

► VIENETTA
BY FLORIS WUBBEN

The name should come as no surprise. Floris Wubben's chair – made from tubular chromed steel and sculptural rolls of white polypropylene sheet – has the distinctive look of Vienetta ice cream. The chair can be taken apart in the event that one or more components need to be replaced. Available in a range of colours.

floriswubben.nl

▲ LASELLA
BY CHIARA CABERLON AND ERMANNO CAROPPI
FOR FORNASARIG

Borrowing techniques used in traditional saddle making, Fornasarig offers customers a chair whose frame has been upholstered to form the perfect basis for well-fitting coverings in fabric or leather. The ultimate comfort provided by LaSella is the result of durable springs made from elastic webbing, variable-density polyurethane foam and polyester fibrefill.

fornasarig.it

◄ STEALTH CHAIR
BY HALDANE MARTIN

A reaction to the current recession, Stealth has an 'aggressive, masculine, armoured form' designed to 'weather the storms of economic instability' according to Haldane Martin, who made the chair from anodized aluminium sheet that was cut and folded using CNC technology. A limited edition of 12 (made for Southern Guild) features etched patterns created by artist Givan Lötz.

haldanemartin.co.za

▲ SHOWTIME LOUNGER
BY JAIME HAYON
FOR BD BARCELONA

With its unmistakable Hayon signature, the Showtime lounge chair is a fusion of classic and contemporary design. The chair, which comes in several colours as well as in walnut, has a striking two-tone effect. Upholstered in fabric or leather.

bdbarcelona.com

▲ TEA
BY ESTUDIHAC JMFERRERO
FOR SANCAL

Embodying the delicacy of an old Chinese tea set, Sancal's Tea collection consists of modular seating elements that can be combined to create surprising configurations. The collection comprises two sofas, an armchair and its smaller brother. Coverings – either smooth or quilted – come in a range of colours and colourways.

sancal.com

◄ FF1
BY FOX AND FREEZE

Made entirely from one square sheet of synthetic felt, the FF1 is self-supporting and is manufactured without wasting material. A couple of holes, some flax rope and a clever twist give the easy chair its asymmetric shape. Available in white, grey, or grey and white.

foxandfreeze.com

▶ WANDERS' TULIP ARMCHAIR
BY MARCEL WANDERS
FOR CAPPELLINI

A fresh and cheerful take on the armchair, Wanders' Tulip has elongated, oversized proportions. The shiny revolving base in dark varnished metal mimics the stem of a flower. Permanent upholstery in a wide range of fabrics.

cappellini.it

▲ MORNING DEW
BY KATI MEYER-BRÜHL
FOR BRÜHL

A cross between green living and floral elegance is Brühl's Morning Dew. Designed to resemble the petals of a flower, the armchair functions as a stand-alone piece but also works well when combined with others to form a group. Upholstery is available in various colours and prints, and the legs are made of wood or aluminium.

bruehl.com

◄ GREY DERIVATIONS
BY MAARTEN BAAS
FOR MITTERRAND+CRAMER

Questioning the idea of creating 'editions', Grey Deviations – which includes a chair, desk, lamp, bookshelf and cabinet – is a collection of unique objects designed by Maarten Baas, who spent literally hundreds of hours in his studio crafting these pieces.

maartenbaas.com

▶ JUMPER
BY BERTJAN POT
FOR ESTABLISHED & SONS

This lounge chair certainly lives up to its name; quirky Jumper wears a removable felted-wool cover that makes it look as though it's donned a jersey. The chair has a frame of powder-coated steel padded in moulded foam. Seat and backrest are made from beech ply. Covers come in grey or grey stripes.

establishedandsons.com

▲ ACHILLE
BY JEAN-MARIE MASSAUD
FOR MDF ITALIA

Providing both visual impact and comfort, Achille comes in two models – with and without armrests – both completely clad in removable covers made from Teflon anti-stain fabric. A version with chrome-plated legs is also available. Achille comes in a variety of eye-catching colours.

mdfitalia.it

▲ CH468
BY HANS WEGNER
FOR CARL HANSEN & SON

The back of the CH468 is upholstered in three sections, giving the chair a sculptural look and providing support to the lower and upper back, neck and shoulders. Its roomy seat and wide armrest covered in foam make for a comfortable lounger. The chair is upholstered in custom fabric.

carlhansen.com

▲ BERTUS
BY ALAIN MONNENS
FOR DURLET

Bertus's most distinguishing feature is its enclosing frame, which is an armrest, a supporting element and an aesthetic detail all in one. Fluid metal 'tubing' – in black, white or dark grey – literally captures the cushions, which carry double ornamental stitching that follows the lines of the overall design.

durlet.com

▲ TORO BADJO
BY IVAN WOODS
FOR SCHIAVELLO

Lounge chair Toro Badjo is a synthesis of Scandinavian design and high functionality. Its wide-angled stance makes it both comfortable and stylish. The cleverly designed chair features a solid-oak frame, leather side panels and contrasting seat and back cushions.

schiavello.com

▲ SCOOP
BY TOM DIXON

Used as a dining chair or side chair, Scoop has one main prerogative: comfort. The chair's generous proportions hold the sitter in an enclosed shell created by applying upholstery to an injection-moulded hard-foam shell. Select from four woven-wool fabrics, and from models with high or low backrests.

tomdixon.net

▲ TIGHT
BY NICOLA GALLIZIA
FOR MOLTENI

Expressing a language similar to that of origami, this armchair is a modern composition of beautifully arranged planes. Tight comes covered in fabric or leather. A footrest completes the picture.

molteni.it

ENGAGING SPACES

EXHIBITION DESIGN EXPLORED

This book offers 30 narrative spaces orchestrated by renowned Dutch exhibition architecture firm Kossmann.dejong. Featured environments range from permanent museums and visitor centres to temporary exhibitions, including the Urbanian Pavilion at the World Expo 2010 in Shanghai. Photos with explanatory texts offer insight into how these spaces are composed while sketches, plans and sections make the designs fully comprehensible. A separate chapter explains 12 basic components of narrative environments. More background information is offered by a 30-page essay on the specialism and an interview with the founders of Kossmann.dejong. *Engaging Spaces* is a must-have sourcebook for everyone interested in narrative environments.

PRICE €34.95 EXCLUDING SHIPPING COSTS

BUY ONLINE AT **FRAMEMAG.COM**

FLORENCE NIGHTINGALE MUSEUM IN LONDON.
PHOTO **THIJS WOLZAK**

◄ ITEM
BY **PATRICK JOUIN**
FOR **BERNHARDT DESIGN**

Ten fully upholstered modules ranging in shape and height define Item, a modular seating system that illustrates the epitome of free-floating design. Backrests vary in height, creating undulating lines. Elements can be combined to form endless seating arrangements.

bernhardtdesign.com

► AIRE
BY **PIERO LISSONI**
FOR **CASSINA**

The modular sofas and armchair belonging to the Aire collection are Cassina's lightest products to date. Made with significantly fewer materials than used for conventional models, the pieces in this collection have removable leather or fabric coverings, reclinable headrests and steel legs, also available with casters.

cassina.com

▼ WILLIAM
BY **DAMIEN WILLIAMSON**
FOR **ZANOTTA**

An armchair, monobloc and modular sofas, a pouf and a day bed make up the William collection, which is characterized by slim aluminium-alloy legs and stacked seating. Removable covers are available in fabric or leather.

zanotta.it

▲ SF05 BESS
BY **STEFAN DIEZ**
FOR **E15**

A seat and backrest flaunting gently rounded forms make Bess an inviting sofa. Base and backrest are made from flexible oak-veneered plywood that is available with a clear- or colour-lacquered finish. The upholstered seat is available in two depths. SF05 Bess is suitable for contract and private use.

e15.com

► XARXA LITT
BY **MARTÍ GUIXÉ**
FOR **DANESE MILANO**

A versatile two- or three-seater sofa, Xarxa Litt has a wooden frame and removable cushions that allow for any number of seating 'interpretations'. Pieces include a chaise longue and sofas with and without armrests. Cushions come in various colours and fabrics.

danesemilano.com

◄ BEBOP
BY **CINI BOERI**
FOR **POLTRONA FRAU**

Simple, pleasantly rounded lines are the focus of this three-seater sofa. Bebop's velvety soft seat envelops the sitter and offers maximum comfort. Leather upholstery in a wide range of colours goes together with tubular-steel feet in either a chrome-plated or gunmetal finish.

poltronafrau.com

Celebrity
MAKE-OVER

JUPITER - BEFORE THE MAKE-OVER!

Just as many stars from the world of film are trying to improve their skills and appearance to maintain their stardom, Jupiter also has undergone a transformation for the better.

The well-known Jupiter has not only been redesigned, but also improved the performance in terms of water saving function, anti-scalding and ceramic regulating system. JUPITER TREND can help you reduce your water consumption by 25-30%

JUPITER TREND meets Damixas design philosophy "When design makes sense" because the series is made in order to beautify and modernize the Jupiter design, to preserve the best features of the classic and adding new environmentally friendly features. A true celebrity makeover...

°C
X-Change
eco-save

JUPITER TREND - at work with the NEW look

JUPITER TREND - Beautiful and practical in the bathroom.

JUPITER TREND - Style in the kitchen. Play with more looks on www.damixa.com

Be inspired by Danish Design...

damixa
When design makes sense

◀ JOE
BY LIEVORE ALTHERR MOLINA
FOR VERZELLONI

Modular and modern, Joe is the name of a seating system comprising a variety of units that promise countless compositional possibilities. One's personal taste can be reflected in an interior landscape displaying different depths and widths. For a more conventional ambience, use Verzelloni's practical hooks to attach armrests to the modules of your choice.

verzelloni.it

▶ FRAME
BY FOERSOM & HIORT-LORENZEN
FOR ERIK JØRGENSEN

Reminiscent of Scandinavian church architecture, Frame boasts crisscross detailing that forms a 'picture frieze' around the back of the sofa. Available as a two- or three-person model. Various types of wood, including birch and oak, complement covers of leather or fabric.

erik-joergensen.com

◀ BABYLON
BY GIORGIO MANZALI
FOR ALBERTA PACIFIC

An aluminium base and a tapered armrest unite to 'lift' the Babylon sofa and provide visual separation from the floor. A high level of comfort is achieved through steel-spring suspension and high-density polyurethane upholstery. Covers are removable.

alberta.it

▶ JALIS
BY JEHS+LAUB
FOR COR

Inspired by the Orient, Jalis is the perfect solution for a relaxed, convivial environment. Delicate patterns woven into fabric coverings are revealed as the light changes. More than simply decoration, cushions are the focal point of this design, which invites users to reconfigure their seating arrangements as desired.

cor.de

▶ BEND SOFA
BY PATRICIA URQUIOLA
FOR B&B ITALIA

Transforming the prevailing concept of a sofa, Bend offers a series of sculptural seats with curvaceous, fluid forms. Urquiola's design features seams in a contrasting colour and an irregular backrest, while never compromising on comfort. The seats are available in a range of sizes and colourways.

bebitalia.com

▶ CHAT
BY CARLO COLOMBO
FOR DE PADOVA

The Chat collection includes two- to four-person sofas, a large armchair and a pouf. Upholstery consisting of goose down and variable-density polyurethane foam cushions the steel frame and drapes to form armrests. The base is available in glossy gunmetal-painted steel or shiny chrome. The removable cover comes in fabric or leather.

depadova.it

Double Vision

firespaces by

safretti ®

www.safretti.com

▶ OTIUM SOFA
BY **MARIO RUIZ**
FOR **LAPALMA**

Otium is a collection of furniture based on this sofa, with its simply curved wooden seat and stainless-steel legs. Because of Ruiz's pared-down form and choice of material, the lightweight object is suitable for both contract and residential use. Otium is available in different types of wood and colours.

lapalma.it

▼ BEE
BY **BJÖRN MULDER**
FOR **PALAU**

Available as a 128-cm-wide two-seater sofa or a 69-cm-wide lounger, the comfortable Bee is an instant invitation to lean back and relax. Bee's stainless-steel frame gives these pieces the look of a modern classic. Available in fabric or leather.

palau.nl

▲ SOFA
BY **JAIME HAYON**
FOR **SÉ**

A stylized shell on slim tubular-steel legs forms the basis of Jaime Hayon's design for the Sé collection. The upholstered frame can be covered in leather, fabric or a combination of the two materials. Legs come in a choice of metallic lacquers or any RAL colour.

se-london.com

◀ RUCHÉ
BY **INGA SEMPÉ**
FOR **LIGNE ROSET**

Interweaving the 'established' with the 'nonconventional', Inga Sempé has come up with a solid-wood base wrapped in a quilted coverlet. Draped over the armrest, the padded seat reveals a wooden base that can be used as a table. Available in various colours and fabrics.

ligneroset.com

◀ BOX
BY **AUTOBAN**

Several sofas and an armchair (pictured here) make up the Box range, which takes its cue from modernist furniture popular in the 1950s. No more than a wooden box before Autoban intervened, this fabric- or leather-upholstered seating collection is ideal for creating a comfortable corner in which to curl up and relax.

autoban212.com

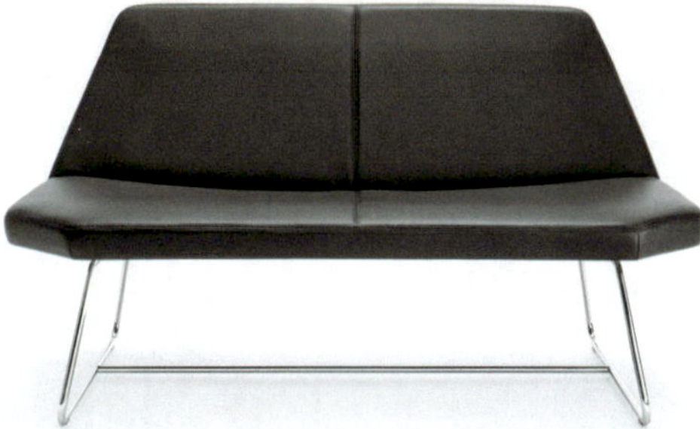

▲ OTTO
BY **CARLOS TÍSCAR**
FOR **GIRSBERGER**

Thanks to connecter sets and tables, the OTTO lounger can be arranged in to form endless configurations. Best suited to public and corporate spaces, the upholstered bench is available in a wide range of fabrics, as well as in leather.

girsberger.com

GOODS

MATERIAL MATTERS

GOODS : 193
MEET EERO AARNIO IN HIS LIGHT AND AIRY HOME ON PAGE 212.
PHOTO TIMO JUNTILLA

GAMFRATESI'S STUDIO, IN A GOVERNMENT-SUBSIDIZED COMPLEX, PROVIDES ACCESS TO A RANGE OF FACILITIES AND SKILLS.

STILL LIVES

With a penchant for slowness, reflection and Danish Modern, is GAMFRATESI succeeding in keeping the frenetic modern world at bay?

WORDS **JANE SZITA**
PHOTOS **CASPER SEJERSEN**

Stine Gam and Enrico Fratesi don't believe in cutting corners. The Danish-Italian designers, collectively known as GamFratesi, are working with quiet intensity in their light-filled studio in Copenhagen, finalizing a clutch of new products: Not Bamboo Lamp, Rewrite (a desk) and a series of small objects still under wraps. The release of all these will mark 2010 as their most prolific year so far, but they're not inclined to rush the process. 'We're not fast,' says Gam. 'We can work for ages on just one thing. Sometimes, it's important to work without a deadline. Speed means you lose quality.'

GamFratesi have spent the last four years producing a handful of products and prototypes that can be read as a quiet paean in praise of such slowness. There's Meduse, a curved-top table with a surface so small that you have to consider carefully what to put on it; Rewrite, a hooded desk that invites you to withdraw into a protective bubble of contemplation; and a range of chairs – Cartoon, Masculo, Alieno, Chameleon – that subtly challenges our expectations of style, seating and sitting. 'We're inviting people to reflect,' says Fratesi. With their well-crafted, minimalist objects, GamFratesi are self-confessed devotees >>>

STINE GAM (LEFT) AND ENRICO FRATESI IN THEIR 18TH-CENTURY STUDIO SPACE. ABOVE THE DESK IS A CLUSTER OF NOT BAMBOO LAMP PROTOTYPES.

THE REWRITE DESK INVITES YOU TO WITHDRAW
INTO A PROTECTIVE BUBBLE OF CONTEMPLATION.

THE SPARE FRAME OF THE MASCULO CHAIR CONTRASTS
WITH ITS MUSCULAR ARMRESTS (SEE OVERLEAF).

THE WOODEN FRAME OF A CHAMELEON CHAIR (LEFT)
ALONGSIDE THE MEDUSE TABLE.

SCALE MODELS OF THE CHAMELEON CHAIR.

'We get annoyed at being called "playful" all the time'
Stine Gam

of the Danish Modern tradition, as exemplified by the likes of Arne Jacobsen, Hans Wegner and Poul Henningsen. 'We're fascinated by the Danish classics,' says Fratesi. 'Although in more recent years design here has been too much about craft,' qualifies Gam. When they won the country's coveted Walk the Plank prize a few months ago, their status as Denmark's most promising young office – as well as hoped-for reinvigorators of the Scandinavian aesthetic – was assured.

They are both quick to remind me that they trained as architects, as did Jacobsen and most of the other Danish masters. They are disapproving of the complete separation of the disciplines that reigns today, and dismissive of much of what now passes for design. 'I don't think we work like most designers,' says Gam.

'We hate mixing up our work with the idea of colour combinations and styling. It's more honest to call what we do "furniture architecture" – that's what Jacobsen and his contemporaries were known as, "furniture architects".'

'We're not just thinking in terms of products, but of how they function in a larger space,' Fratesi elaborates. 'And our work is architectural in the way we approach line, detail and technical elements. We're not just gluing things together. We like to show how they are connected. We can really freak out about the details.' A good example is the Masculo chair, with its curiously curved armrests that had to be expensively hand-finished. 'The manufacturer [Gubi] wasn't too happy about the costs, but they agreed with us that we needed to retain the clean shape,' he says. 'The other solutions were just ugly.'

Building detailed prototypes for manufacturers is part and parcel of GamFratesi's patiently painstaking design process. 'We like to resolve all the finishing as part of the design,' says Gam. This entails working with skilled craftsmen or learning the crafts themselves: for the new series of small objects, she studied the techniques of wood turning. Access to workshops and facilities like these is one of the advantages of their splendid 18th-century studio space in a government-subsidized warehouse complex (called Statens Verksteder for Kunst og Handverk) for artists and craftworkers. 'We couldn't work like this without this place,' says Gam. 'It's a wonderful luxury.'

They distrust computer-design tools, 'although it's impossible to avoid them completely', says Fratesi. 'But for us, >>>

THE CARVED ARMRESTS OF THE MASCULO CHAIR HAD
TO BE HAND-FINISHED – AN EXPENSIVE UNDERTAKING.

'We're inviting people to reflect'
Enrico Fratesi

everything starts with a freehand sketch.' As we talk, the duo frequently explain themselves by putting a drawing under my nose or pointing to a sketch on the wall. 'The drawing has to embody the essence of the idea,' says Gam. The link between sketch and finished object is made explicit in the name of the Cartoon chair, which even in its polished final form (manufactured by Swedese) exudes a studied spontaneity. 'The concept and expression stayed the same; only the proportions were tweaked,' says Gam. 'We could never have arrived at this result with a rendering.'

With its oversized back and mismatched buttons, Cartoon illustrates how GamFratesi frequently seek to update the Scandinavian design values that they've adopted by subverting them. 'Generally, we're looking for an element

of disharmony,' says Fratesi. 'We try to find that turning point where something unexpected occurs, and it surprises. We want our objects to trigger a kind of recognition, but with a jolt of the unfamiliar.' In the monochrome Chameleon chair, released this year by manufacturer Erik Jørgensen, such a point is provided by the padded backrest that discreetly disturbs the strict simplicity of the wooden chair.

Adding a layer of richness to the Danish basis of GamFratesi's output is a dash of Italian bravura – the designers often work for extended periods in Italy and constantly speak the language to each other – in the theoretical and conceptual underpinning of their work, as well as in their devotion to making things for production: 'We're not doing one-off art pieces,' says Gam. There are touches of flamboyance, too, times >>>

GAMFRATESI'S CHAIRS (FROM LEFT, MASCULO, ANTROPOMORFO, CHAMELEON AND CARTOON) ARE THE RESULT OF SEARCHING FOR 'AN ELEMENT OF DISHARMONY'.

WINNING THE WALK THE PLANK PRIZE ASSURED GAMFRATESI'S STATUS AS DENMARK'S MOST PROMISING YOUNG OFFICE.

There are touches of flamboyance, times when GamFratesi's work is more Starck than stark

'I'M VERY ITALIAN, VERY ENERGETIC, AND STINE IS VERY CALM AND SCANDINAVIAN,' SAYS FRATESI (RIGHT).

when their work is more Starck than stark: the anthropomorphism, the playing with scale, the funny names.

'I'm very Italian, very energetic, and Stine is very calm and Scandinavian,' says Fratesi. 'We both suffer, but she does it in a quieter way.' Because of their bicultural origins and their experiences of working in Japan and Sweden respectively, they are, says Gam, 'obsessed with contrasts, and forced to analyse everything all the time. The problem is we don't divide tasks. We started out with different skill sets, but now we do everything together. We sit in front of the same computer, sometimes fighting over the mouse. We spend a lot of time discussing, arguing, trying to convince each other.'

They take their work very seriously. 'We get annoyed at being called "playful" all the time,'

says Gam. 'This isn't a joke. We're not setting out to be funny.' 'We believe in the social importance of design,' adds Fratesi. 'As we spend 90 per cent of our time doing it, we have to be convinced that it matters. Our work is expressing our view of society, and hopefully we can change society in small ways.' Gam sighs: 'There's so much bad design around. It's just used to sell things. We're living in the age of marketing.'

Perhaps the key to GamFratesi's work is its reconciliation of a certain contemporary pop sensibility (or what Gam calls the 'friendly' quality of their work) with a nostalgia for pre-digital days – a time when the world was still the logical, material realm of modernism, when design, rather than selling products, was a feature of things that worked properly, when a piece of furniture could last a lifetime, and

when the person who made that furniture could still be called 'an architect'. The apparent pursuit of authenticity is already winning GamFratesi considerable recognition. 'Since we won the prize, we've been getting more attention and a lot of new opportunities,' says Fratesi. It will be interesting to see where they go from here, and how their growing success will affect the intense one-on-one collaboration that has proved the strength of their work so far. Will popularity weaken their rejection of much of contemporary consumerist design? 'Our society produces too much too quickly,' says Gam. 'Designers are pressurized to keep producing. It's hard to resist if you want to maintain your own tempo.' Who knows how long GamFratesi will be able to keep going slow? ▬

gamfratesi.com

YVES BÉHAR SKETCHES A POTENTIAL PATTERN FOR SAYL'S BACKREST.

PUT TO THE TEST

HERMAN MILLER's SAYL, designed by YVES BÉHAR, might well be the world's first frameless chair – but it's the price that will most delight the deskbound.

WORDS **SHONQUIS MORENO**
PHOTOS **COURTESY OF FUSEPROJECT**

'We started with a large set of questions rather than a brief,' says Yves Béhar of fuseproject about his design of the SAYL task chair for Herman Miller. 'Is it possible to build a high-performance, lighter-weight, recyclable, low-cost task chair with less plastic, fewer parts, more finish options and a standard 12-year, 24-hour, 3-shift-use Herman Miller warranty?' The answer, after two years, appears to be yes.

With its price point, material efficiency and quality, SAYL revives the ideal of affordability embodied by the Eames 1946 moulded plywood chair. HM's wildly successful 15-year-old Aeron chair costs just under $900 (approximately €700); SAYL retails for under $400 (€312). At that price, you typically get a black chair assembled from off-the-shelf components. SAYL, however, offers options like a translucent

backrest or, flamboyant by comparison with most office slings, a red back paired with mulberry upholstery. And the product also heads a household of five members, which includes a cantilevering side chair that the design team refers to as 'the little black dress'.

A small chair, perhaps, but no small task. The family launched from every direction at the same time this October – to the contract and consumer markets, nationally and internationally – as well as retailing online. Fuseproject calls SAYL 'a frameless chair', and if you're picturing a picture-frame frame you've got the idea of what they've left out. Structural support comes from a two-part suspension (spine-and-pelvis) system. It leaves no hard edges around the back, provides a responsive 'living' surface calibrated to target support precisely and offers the torso

greater freedom of movement. Freedom is a fine way to describe fuseproject's creative concept, which the studio dubs 'unframed'. For the first time since HM's halcyon years under the leadership of George Nelson, Béhar has done end-to-end design – if not directed it – from brand strategy and art direction to industrial design and packaging. Like the Mercedes-Benz Smart car or the BMW Mini, SAYL was positioned as a product capable of reinvigorating a mature company and raising the market's low expectations surrounding the quality of low-cost products.

That's a lot of pressure for a little chair, but SAYL can bear the weight. The chair is built like a bridge, and the teams have used bridge-suspension terminology to talk about it. The spine-like Y-shaped 'tower' is moulded from >>>

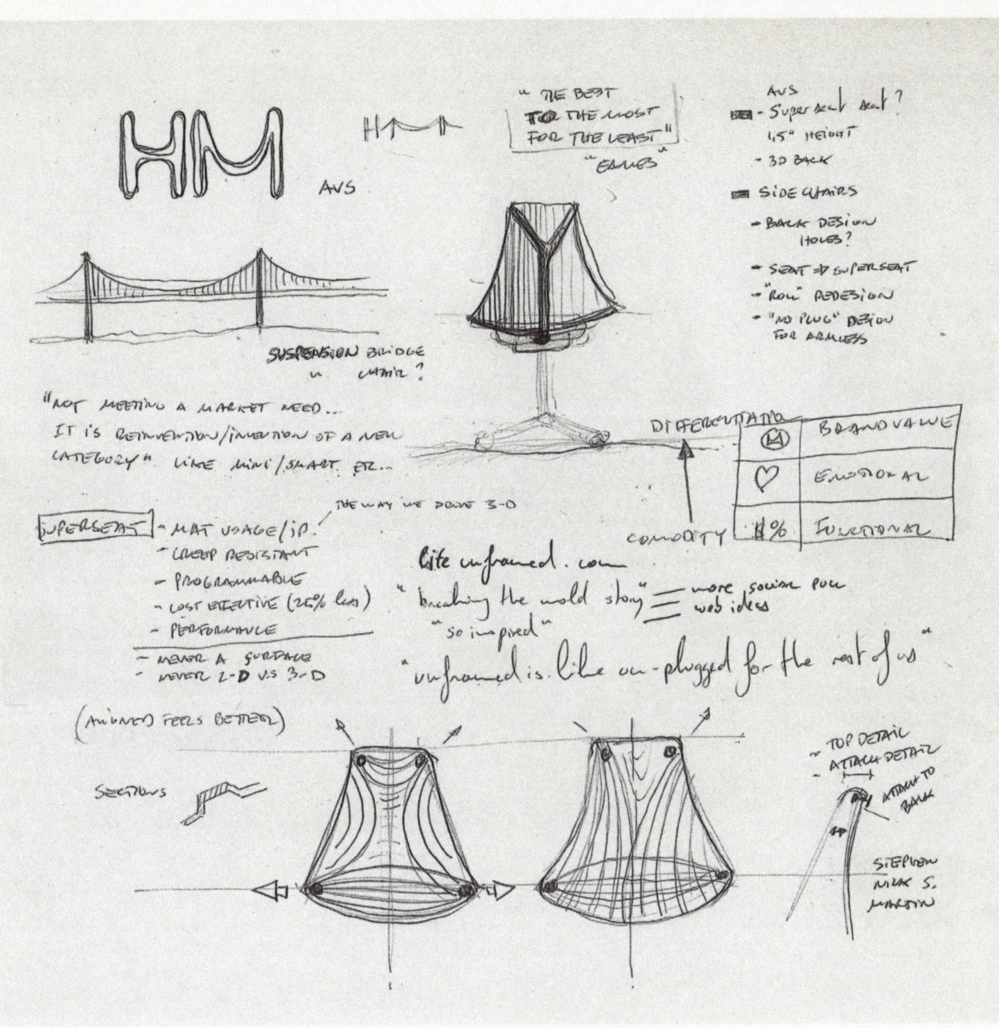

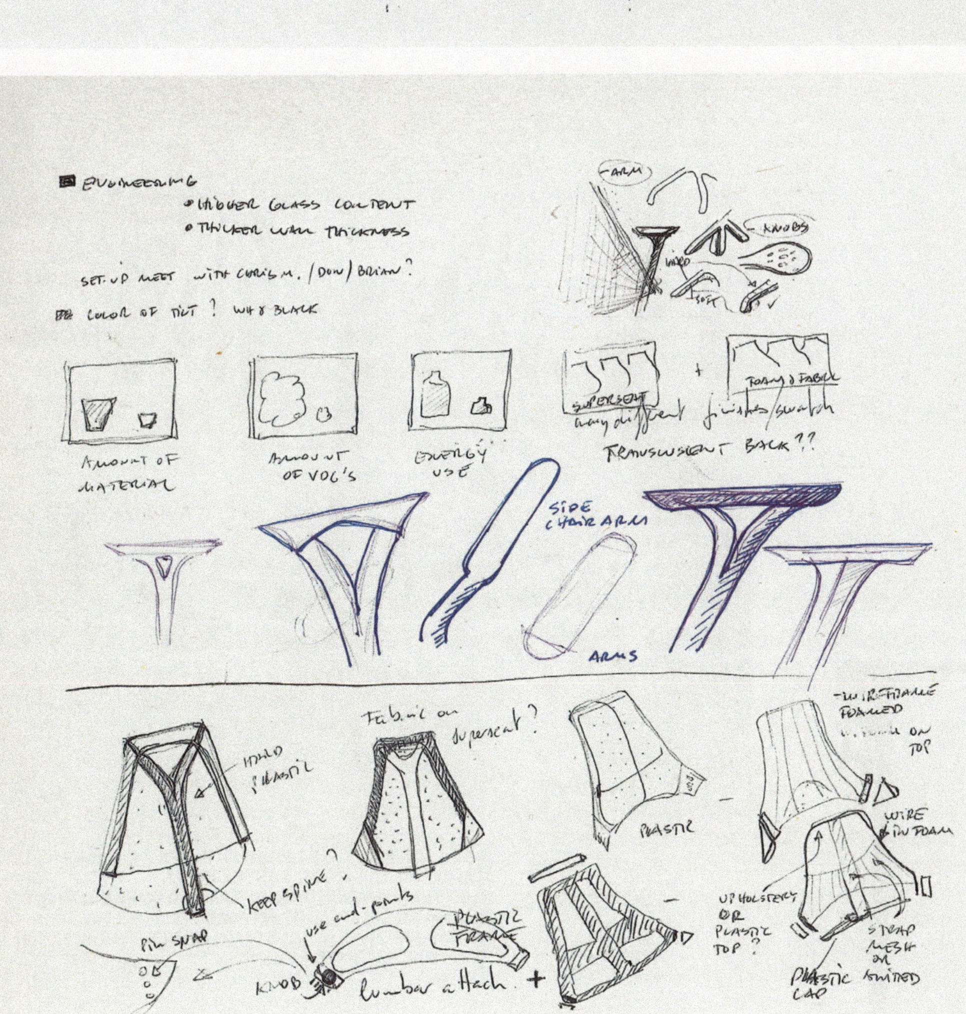

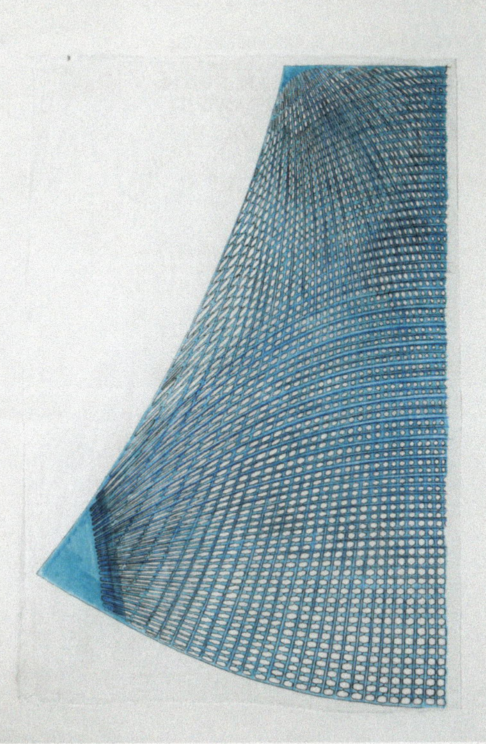

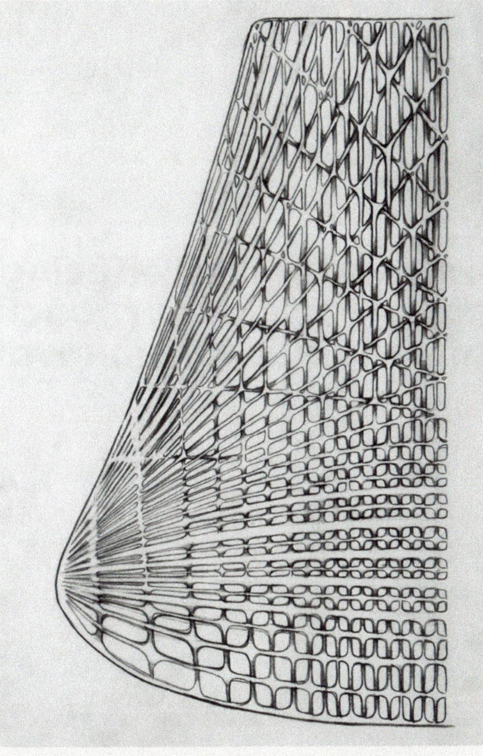

SOME OF THE HUNDREDS OF HAND-DRAWN SKETCHES THAT BÉHAR MADE WHILE EXPLORING DIFFERENT PATTERNS FOR THE SAYL BACKREST.

INITIAL DRAWINGS FROM YVES BÉHAR'S SKETCHBOOK SHOW THE INFLUENCE OF SUSPENSION BRIDGES IN THE DESIGN OF SAYL.

YVES BÉHAR (LEFT) AND BRET RECOR, DIRECTOR OF TECHNICAL DESIGN AT FUSEPROJECT, EXAMINE A PROTOTYPE WHILE CONSIDERING THE FEASIBILITY OF A WOVEN BACK.

'Instead of just reducing costs, you can approach affordability via innovation'
Don Goeman

SUSPENDING PROTOTYPES OF THE BACKREST ENABLED THE TEAM TO FEEL, TEST AND SEE HOW THEY REACTED TO STRETCHING.

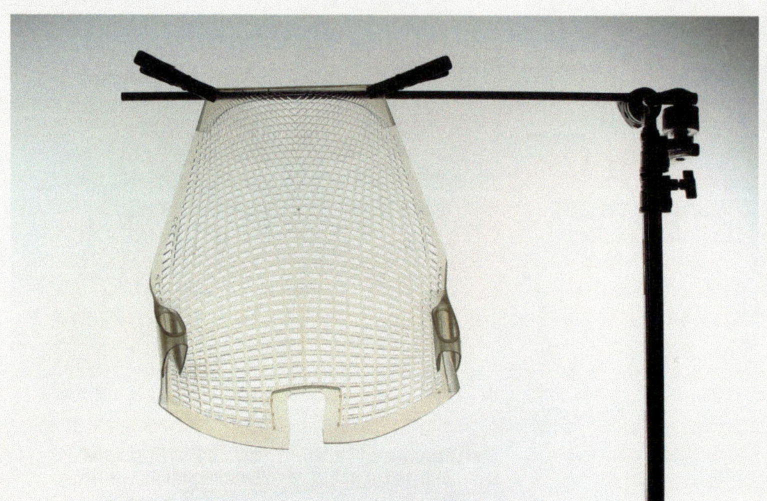

INITIAL MOCK-UPS WERE MADE WITH ROPE AND DESIGNED TO FOLLOW THE ERGONOMICS OF THE HUMAN BODY. AS SHOWN HERE, THE SHAPE WAS THEN RE-CREATED USING URETHANE-ELASTOMER STRAPS. THIS APPROACH ALLOWED FOR AN EASY ADJUSTMENT OF THE STRAPS, WITHOUT THE NEED FOR EXPENSIVE MACHINES.

TWO PROTOTYPES FROM DIFFERENT STAGES OF THE CHAIR'S DEVELOPMENT SHOW THE EVOLUTION OF THE BACKREST. EARLY ON, A STRING VERSION WITH GREEN DOTS (LEFT) WAS USED TO MODEL PRESSURE POINTS. THE LATER VERSION (RIGHT) SHOWS THE DEVELOPMENT OF THE SAIL.

A CLOSE-UP OF A PROTOTYPE OF THE BACKREST – MADE FROM A SHEET OF MATERIAL WITH LASER-CUT OPENINGS – SHOWS ONE ITERATION OF THE PATTERN.

glass-reinforced plastic. An 'arc span', in the same material, belts the back of the seat like the bones of the pelvis. The meticulously engineered backrest, called the sail, features strands of varying thickness and tensile strength made from injection-moulded urethane elastomer ('with a special sauce'). The sail is stretched by a hydraulic machine between the prongs of the tower and the arc span where it becomes taut but responsive. (The first attempted stretching took a nail-tapping 45 minutes.) In early sketches the mesh was woven; later it became seamless but uneven, and the height, width and depth of each strand were tweaked and re-tweaked. 'We sweated fractions of a millimetre in making this product work,' reports Brent Tracy, the manager of product-development engineering who, until 1994, worked in aerospace. 'I'd say the sail was

three times more complex than any part we've previously done.'

It was Nike who first introduced Béhar to Herman Miller. By 2006 the company had premiered his ribbon-like Leaf Light, and in October 2008 the two 'set SAYL' together. Since then, the design has been subjected to a lengthy, meticulous and costly design/build/test loop. Initially, fuseproject FTPed obsessively detailed exploratory sketches to HM engineers in the form of STEP or IGES files. Over hundreds of hours, HM translated this formal data into mathematics-based structural files in AnSys, Pro/Engineer and CAD. Lengthy multidisciplinary brainstorming sessions were conducted in the bachelor-pad-like Project Room – an explosion of whiteboards, furniture fragments and overflowing cabinets – resulting in the first crude prototype. Its backrest

was threaded with string held together by green tape, and its seat was gloopy with resin.

'We were trying to probe what was missing at this price point instead of asking what we could take out,' Tracy explains. One thing they did take out was material. Less weight, less plastic and fewer parts make the chair more environmentally friendly and less expensive. This dematerialization meant, for instance, hollowing out the tension adjustor into two graceful spokes. The arm stems, raised and lowered via a ratchet mechanism, have no active controls – thus no extra parts – and a satisfying haptic click with each adjustment (whose volume they strove to lower, however). Where there are controls, they are relatively light and refined. Even the Y tower and arc span have grooves that make them as minimal as they are structural. And structural >>>

THE SAYL BEING 'TORTURED' IN HERMAN MILLER'S TEST LAB. A WEIGHT IS PLACED ON THE SEAT, AND THE BACKREST IS ATTACHED TO STRAPS THAT PULL IT BACKWARDS.

THE SPINE-LIKE, Y-SHAPED 'TOWER' AWAITING ASSEMBLY. GROOVES REDUCE WEIGHT AND MATERIAL USAGE.

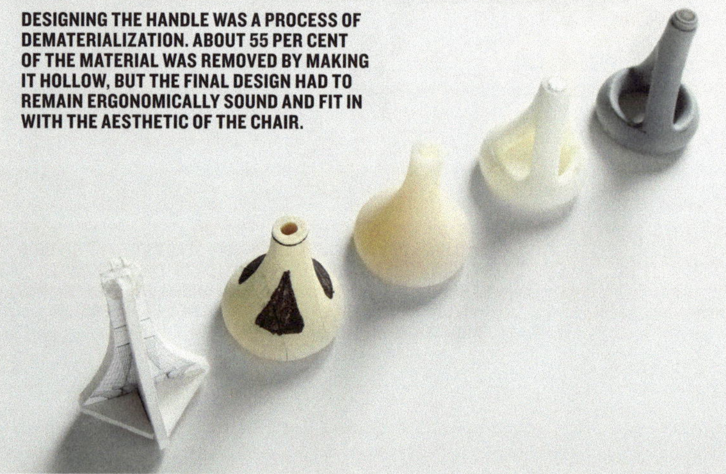

DESIGNING THE HANDLE WAS A PROCESS OF DEMATERIALIZATION. ABOUT 55 PER CENT OF THE MATERIAL WAS REMOVED BY MAKING IT HOLLOW, BUT THE FINAL DESIGN HAD TO REMAIN ERGONOMICALLY SOUND AND FIT IN WITH THE AESTHETIC OF THE CHAIR.

'We sweated fractions of a millimetre in making this product work'
Brent Tracy

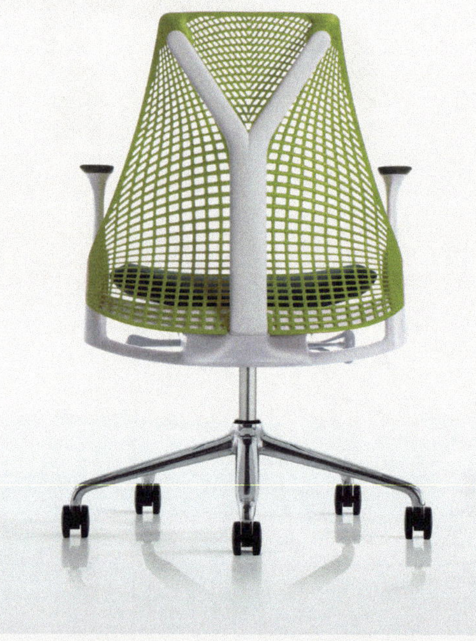

BACK VIEW OF THE FINAL CHAIR, SHOWING OFF ITS FRAMELESS FORM.

they are: engineers raised the load limit from the industry-dictated 300 to 350 lbs (136 to 159 kg) and ensured that SAYL would ship in a box roughly half its assembled size.

HM conducts tests in a series of bright, high-ceilinged rooms in the West Michigan headquarters that Béhar has nicknamed 'Where Designers' Dreams Go To Die' and which others simply call 'The Graveyard'. This is the Test Lab in which SAYL weathered 200 tests (as do all HM chairs) and where the mantra is 'Trust but Verify'. Tests are carried out on both new and existing products – in one corner of the room, a Leaf Light has been switched on and off since 2006 to measure LED durability – by both industry-standard and custom-designed machines. Assembly lines on the factory floor are also purpose-designed for each product.

The Aeron and Mirra lines are, indeed, linear; SAYL's 'line' has a horseshoe configuration that will be refined continually over the first year of manufacture. Engineers pressed the limits of durability, safety and ergonomics of the SAYL and its parts as measured by three sets of international standards. They also focused on the intricate geometry of the back. The machines – with their generic anatomies: thick arms and legs and faces animated by gauges – do everything from load tests, using shot bags, and vibration tests that simulate truck transport to drop testing in the package and on the pallet. More subjective comfort testing is based on feedback gathered from people, at the company and elsewhere, who use the chairs in four-hour increments. Testing often exceeds standards: SAYL's backrest was severely stressed one million times, or cycles,

in a 'cyclic durability test'; North American standards require only 150,000 cycles.

In the end, more than 70 large-scale prototypes (not to mention parts) were fabricated. This is a conservative estimate, and it means that SAYL's cost of production is inversely proportional to its retail cost. 'Instead of just hunkering down and reducing costs,' insists Don Goeman, executive vice president of research, design and development, 'you can approach affordability via innovation. This is the more noble, and the more challenging, use of design.' ∎

fuseproject.com

FRONT VIEW OF THE COMPLETED SAYL CHAIR, WITH RED
BACKREST, MULBERRY FABRIC SEAT AND GREY FRAME.

DESIGNERS NEED CRITICS

As long as the specialist design press functions as a glorified PR service, argues RICK POYNOR, the mainstream will continue to treat design as a lightweight consumer subject – to the detriment of us all, not least the designers among us.

TOO MUCH DESIGN WRITING EXISTS ONLY IN THE FAST-EVAPORATING MOMENT

It is curious that in 2010 the idea of design criticism remains such an issue. Design has been a matter of serious discussion in Europe since the Second World War. Bruno Munari's wonderfully fresh critical reflections on design, now back in print, were written in the 1960s. Reyner Banham, one of the greatest design writers and still a model for aspiring design critics, also made his mark in that decade of accelerating change. For the last 30 years design has been a hot and increasingly public topic. During the 'design boom' of the 1980s, when I landed a writing job on *Blueprint* in London, I couldn't believe my good fortune. Many of the best design and architecture critics of the day – Deyan Sudjic (*Blueprint*'s editor), Stephen Bayley, Peter York, Martin Pawley, James Woudhuysen, Janet Abrams, Jonathan Glancey, Rowan Moore – wrote for the magazine. Nobody ever needed to say that writing was important, that it should be sharp, textured, closely observed and critical, that it was a reason for buying *Blueprint*, or that it deserved plenty of space. That was all self-evident.

Yet today a huge question mark hangs over design criticism. Is it needed? What does it have to offer? How many readers even want it? Designers sometimes complain that design magazines aren't sufficiently critical. Then, if they happen to find their own work on the receiving end of even the mildest criticism, they yelp with dismay at the perceived injustice. I have seen this myself. A couple of outspoken design superstars I had the temerity to criticize in the 1990s refused to speak to me for many years. Such easily bruised egos, such astonishingly thin skins. Editors and publishers must defend their

ethical and intellectual right to publish reasoned and fair critical comment on a field that can only benefit from the careful examination of new ideas, trends, received wisdoms and fads. What is meaningful and valuable now, and what isn't? If critical inquiry was continuous and normal, the design profession would gain immeasurably in critical self-awareness, sense of social purpose and public understanding.

Some believe it is already too late. There is a persistent claim that if criticism hasn't given up the ghost already, then it is drawing its last breath. A recent collection of writings by the late Martin Pawley, a titan among architecture critics, serves notice in its title on *The Strange Death of Architectural Criticism*. Joe Clark, a Canadian blogger, has a category devoted to 'The death of graphic-design criticism' where he tolls the bell for this allegedly moribund practice with gleeful relish. An earlier essay I wrote about design writing for *Icon* magazine went out with title 'The Death of the Critic' – not quite my intention. And design criticism isn't alone in hastening the last rites. Critics of literature, film and art agonise over whether their much longer established and more publicly accessible trades are coming to an end.

It is too easy to say that this is all down to the way that the online environment has changed our information-gathering and reading habits. In the 1990s, before the Internet was even an issue, there was already a widespread assumption in magazine publishing that 'readers' had less patience or inclination to read and that magazines needed to become more visual, with more pictures and more intricate page design. *Blueprint*, then in the hands of a different

editorial team, began to reduce the length of its articles. This self-defeating move was a troubling sign for anyone who understood that ambitious critical writing needs space, but it rapidly became the new wisdom among magazine-makers convinced their audiences were more likely to scan and graze than to engage in attentive reading. Looking at almost any kind of magazine from the 1960s today is a shock: there are so many towering columns of words to take in.

There can be no doubt, though, that the Internet has had a profound impact on design magazines with inevitable consequences for the way they handle critical writing – if it matters to them at all. As readers abandon print or just never acquire the habit, many advertisers are no longer convinced that this is the way to reach them. The economic downturn intensified the pain. The most alarming events have been the closure in December 2009 of *I.D.* magazine after 55 years as the leading American design title, followed in June this year by the sudden demise of the British magazine *Grafik*, which until then had appeared to be thriving. Other titles, such as *Metropolis* in New York, look worryingly malnourished. Advertising has dried up, the page count has fallen and the long critical reviews it once published have been dropped. *Icon*'s earlier commitment to 3,000-word critical essays is another casualty of leaner, recessionary times.

These magazines still show plenty of pictures, of course, but as a long-term survival strategy this seems inadequate since the Internet will win every time when it comes to delivering instantly available new images. Even the superior quality of print won't in the end be enough. The same >>>

DESIGN RECEIVES A CONSISTENTLY EASY RIDE IN THE SPECIALIST PRESS

goes for industry news and topical comment, which blogs are better positioned to provide. Design magazines' online presence, on the other hand, often looks half-hearted – *I.D.* was left standing by web competitors such as *Core77*, *Designboom* and *Dezeen*. Magazine sites and blogs exist in an uneasy relationship with the parent publication and brand they are supposed to support and promote, diverting resources that were previously focused entirely on producing the printed page. They look like transitional ventures, place holders waiting for the moment when the burdensome weight of the paper magazine can finally be cut away and abandoned because the online world has found a way of properly monetizing Internet-based publishing.

Core77 publishes well-written essays and reviews, as does *Design Observer*, but the online world has not seen the outbreak of compelling new critical voices in design one might have expected – writing equal to the insight and panache of Pawley, Sudjic or Bayley in their prime. Dare one suggest, then, that probing critical commentary and analysis by knowledgeable writers is one area where magazines still have the potential to supply something valuable that's not easily found elsewhere. The more pictures come to dominate a design magazine's pages, the less it will look like a writer's – or a reader's – medium. To stand any chance of commanding attention, the text needs a strong graphic presence of its own (1980s' *Blueprint* managed this awkward image/text balancing act with aplomb). It is also worth noting that the dependence of design magazines on pictures supplied or authorized by a project's

clients and designers has frequently limited their writers' power to comment freely on what the pictures show.

For the sake of argument, let's say we did have a fully mature design criticism in the design press. What would it look like and what would it be doing? First of all, it would need to find a way of staying close to its subject while maintaining a sceptical distance. This is not easy to pull off. Journalism is a good starting point because a journalist has access. Only by meeting the key figures, going behind closed doors and seeing things from the inside is it possible to gain a real sense of the milieu. (Designers who turn to writing have an initial advantage – they already inhabit this world – but naturally then find it difficult, if not impossible, to achieve detachment; they worry too much about their design colleagues' reactions to what they write.)

One would expect writers in any field to be passionately engaged with their subject and to keep surprising us with their knowledge. We take this for granted in political writing in the press where commentators show a detailed command of recent political history: what happened when, who said what, and how it relates to what's happening now. When I started, the best design writers brought wide experience and hard-won insight to their writing, making it denser, richer and more convincing. This kind of knowledge is rarer now in design. Forever frothing with excitement about the latest thing, too much design writing exists only in the fast-evaporating moment; it lacks a cultural memory and shows no sign of realizing what it doesn't know. Without a close understanding of context and the ability this brings to make comparisons and arrive

at carefully weighed judgements, a subtle, sophisticated criticism is simply not possible.

Another crucial point about criticism is that it needs to be genuinely critical. This is taken for granted in other kinds of cultural reviewing and criticism: films, novels, plays, art exhibitions and music are all subject to continuous evaluation (though these consumer-orientated assessments also have their flaws). The reader's awareness that adverse criticism is not only possible but merciless when necessary gives favourable judgements more reliability and weight. By contrast, design receives a consistently easy ride in the specialist press, which often seems to aspire to be nothing more than a glamorous PR platform and support service, while general media, with no other model of design discussion to go on, treat design as a lightweight consumer subject in the style and lifestyle pages. Not for the first time, we need to remind ourselves that there can be no serious, well-informed, mainstream design criticism if design publishing has not already set a high standard of critical inquiry to show how it should be done. Design is a fusion of commerce and culture. For design criticism to develop, we need to place a great deal more emphasis on investigating the cultural implications of that union.

If design criticism remains an ideal more talked about than engaged in, there have still been some notable educational initiatives of late. In 2008, new Master's degree courses in design writing and criticism started at the London College of Communication and at the School of Visual Arts in New York. The Konstfack design school in Stockholm also runs an MA in critical writing and curatorial practice. In October,

THE MORE PICTURES DOMINATE A DESIGN MAGAZINE'S PAGES, THE LESS IT LOOKS LIKE A WRITER'S – OR A READER'S – MEDIUM

another design and art criticism MA opens its doors at the Royal College of Art in London. For anyone who believes that criticism could have an important role to play, courses exploring its methods and applications can only be a positive development. The obvious question to ask next is: Where do these graduates expect to find work in a shrinking field? (This might change in time.) And assuming they do find viable places to write, what do they and their teachers, for that matter, understand the purpose of design criticism to be?

Alice Twemlow, chair of SVA's D-Crit course, provides one possible answer to the question of purpose in a recent post for *Design Observer* titled 'Howling at the Moon: The Poetics of Amateur Product Reviews'. Designers of all kinds are finding new ways to involve design's end-users, ordinary people, in the design process and Twemlow approaches design criticism from the same angle. Analysing the often hilarious user reviews on Amazon.com of a self-flushing cat toilet and a T-shirt with a howling wolf motif, she proposes that this kind of imaginative user feedback is 'not a deviation from the true path of design criticism but, rather, a logical extension of a democratizing impulse that has always been at its core'. She goes on to argue that the mighty Reyner Banham anticipated these developments in his accessible critical writing about everyday subjects and 'empowered the casual and independent observer to comment on their own designed environment'. This, Twemlow believes, is a key task for the 21st-century design critic: to educate and encourage design's users by generous example. 'Criticism is only really productive,' she concludes, 'if it reaches its intended audience in a way that surprises,

goads or otherwise convinces them to act.' I wouldn't put it as baldly as this. Who is to say, after all, what is 'productive' and what isn't? Why is it so important to act? And what constitutes an act, anyway? In the context of a product review, does acting mean buying something? Deciding not to buy something on the basis of a bad review would be a non-act, though still a positive, active decision. Is criticism only fully productive if it inspires readers to compose reviews of their own? Why isn't simply thinking and reflecting enough? Twemlow's efficiency-driven argument looks like a bid for certainty, a desire for an objective, measurable outcome, where certainty is neither achievable nor necessary.

The truth, I would suggest, is that excellent criticism will always find readers and those readers will use it in whatever ways they need. All the committed critic has to worry about – no easy task – is trying to do the best possible job. As for the reader, the most trenchant response, never more so than now, is to encourage criticism's continuing existence by supporting the platforms that provide it. Good critical writing is vital to the design field, to any cultural field, in a looser, less easy to quantify sense that can be best apprehended through our own histories and experiences as readers. Criticism prises open doors, reveals unforeseen possibilities, enhances our awareness, refines our values, hones our taste and exerts a myriad of influences on the judgements, decisions and actions we will take in the future. Whether we are fully conscious of this web of inspiration or not, criticism helps to shape our mentality. ▬

EERO'S ERA

In his light and spacious villa just outside Helsinki, designer EERO AARNIO talks about his latest chair, old saunas and designs of the future.

WORDS **FEMKE DE WILD**
PHOTOS **TIMO JUNTILLA**

Finland is known for Alvar Aalto's modern architecture, Artek's functionalist furniture, Iitala's stunning glassware and long, dark days. In the sombre world of Europe's most northerly regions, Eero Aarnio's villa is an oasis of light and colour. The same can be said of his products. The bright-red Tomato chair he designed in 1971 stands in the lush, green garden, and the glazed entrance to the house – also of his own creation – could be mistaken for a showroom, thanks to the presence of Aarnio's often vividly hued designs in fibreglass and plastic.

Aarnio is standing in front of a small wooden building at the rear of the garden, which borders a large lake. 'The idea for this smoke sauna is a very old one, but it's also the best,' he says. 'The temperature inside can get up to 130 degrees centigrade; I spent some time inside just yesterday.' He points to an ancient rock next to the sauna as he walks up the slope to the house. Hanging in the middle of the light-filled living room is the first prototype of his new Ring chair. The hovering seat balances on a solid ring attached to the ceiling by means of a sturdy chain. 'Take a seat. You've got to sit in it,' says the enthusiastic 78-year-old designer, who's obviously still in the thick of things. >>>

'I'M VERY GRATEFUL TO PLAYBOY,' JOKES AARNIO, REFERRING TO THE SLIDING PARTITION IN THE LIVING ROOM, A SURFACE CLAD IN MAGAZINE COVERS. HE DESIGNED THE PONY CHAIRS (FOREGROUND) IN 1973.

HANGING ON THE WALL ARE FRAMED CROSSWORD PUZZLES FROM THE NEW YORK TIMES. THE CORRECT ANSWER TO ONE CLUE – 'INNOVATIVE FURNITURE DESIGNER AARNIO' – IS EERO.

'I ALWAYS MAKE FULL-SCALE DRAWINGS,' SAYS AARNIO, LEANING OVER HIS WORKTABLE AND EXAMINING A RECENT DRAWING OF THE RING CHAIR.

DINO, A DESIGN FROM 2009, IS MANUFACTURED BY FINNISH COMPANY MELAJA.

'Every young designer should have to design, build and pay for a house'
Eero Aarnio

The Ring chair reminds me of the Bubble chair you designed in 1968 – does it represent a return to your early years?
I drew a sketch of the chair on 31 December 2008 and just finished this prototype, but the idea dates back a good 40 years. I travel crisscross through time in my thoughts. For me, time isn't linear. An idea from the distant past can suddenly surface in my mind, usually because it couldn't be implemented at the time it first struck me. My work is based on the principle of achieving a maximum of strength and a maximum effect with a minimum of material. Everybody wants to do that. People are lazy by nature. In the 1960s I opted for rounded forms for the simple reason that those shapes were the best and most economical way to make objects out of fibreglass. But not all my designs feature rounded forms, even though everyone seems to think so.

Your designs from the 1960s were often seen as a reflection of the spirit of the times. The rounded forms were said to symbolize early space travel, experimentation, optimism and pop art.
That's all somebody else's idea. For me the 1960s were primarily a time of great economic hardship. I'd just stopped working at the factory, had recently married and had two small children. How was I to survive? That was my biggest problem. I worked as a professional photographer for architecture magazines, did graphic design for advertising agencies and designed interiors. I did just about everything in order to earn money, when all I really wanted to do was design products.

What made you set your sights on that, of all things?
I don't know. It's just what I wanted to do. Why are you a journalist? During the war I was already crafting wooden aeroplanes. Later I made boats. Gradually, the things I made grew in size. I remember putting together the first Pony, somewhere outdoors. I made the model from clay and polystyrene foam. I still find those little white pellets fluttering around in the forest. Nowadays I draw all my designs by hand, on paper, full scale. I no longer have to construct models, because I have a mental image of the object in its entirety – in three dimensions. I think in three dimensions. It all happens in my mind. My brain is my computer.

So the computer hasn't influenced your work?
I draw everything by hand, but in another way the computer has indeed made my life much easier. Working with manufacturers in other countries, for example, has become much simpler. I can email my sketches to them. Another big advantage is the growing opportunity to sell products over the internet. You ought to interview Mia Lewin, the owner of DesignStory. What she's doing is the future. She's out to make the link between factory and consumer as short as possible by selling products exclusively online. That way she keeps the costs of storage and logistics low.

Logistics are very important. It's this kind of thinking that gave birth to the Pastil chair. When I had to ship the Ball chair, I ended up sending a carton that was half empty. So I decided to design a chair that would fit into the unfilled cavity. Designers have to think of everything. You have to know how a mould is made, how many components it can have before the design becomes far too expensive, how a product will be transported, what market segment you're targeting. That's the good thing about being my age – you know how things work.

What's the best way to learn how things work?
Every young designer should have to design, build and pay for a house. I've moved up >>>

'People talk too much about design'
Eero Aarnio

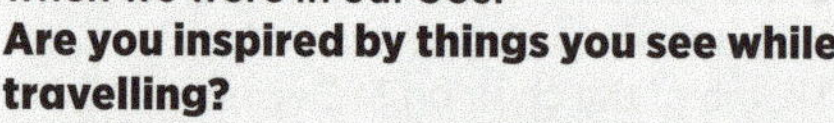

GLASS WAS USED FOR THE FIRST MODELS
OF THE DOUBLE BUBBLE LAMP, WHICH IS
CURRENTLY MADE FROM PLASTIC.

the housing ladder, step by step, each time into a bigger house, until finally getting to the stage where I could pay for this house outright. I didn't have to borrow a cent. Building a house is the best school a designer can have. It helps you to appreciate the work of others, because you need a lot of people to get the job done. When you buy an existing house, you don't know what you're getting. A house is a kind of machine; it's got to work. I started by considering where the garage should be, especially with an eye to winter, when you want your car to have the least hindrance from snow. Where do you want the kitchen, the place where you have to lug all the groceries? Where should the sun be when you have time to relax? This house works.

Is the same true of design? Is it best when it works?
'Design' is the wrong word. It's used for everything today. No longer is a distinction made between styling and design. Above all else, good design is design that's been well considered. If it takes two hours to change a light bulb, the lamp hasn't been well designed. A design should be easy to produce, environmentally sound and affordable. Good design is like a puzzle. This definition never changes; it's been the same for the past hundred years. The match and the wheel are perfect examples of great design.
People talk too much about design. I don't like talking about it. That's why I've never given courses or held lectures on the subject. I prefer to develop new ideas. After I showed my design for the Ball chair to Asko, it was kept secret from certain members of the board. Someone said, 'If we sell even one of those chairs, I'll eat my hat.' The very first year the chair became an immediate commercial success, because nothing else like it existed.

Where do you get the motivation needed to make one new product after another?
I don't know why I make what I make. It's not easy to talk about immaterial things. Why does the E in the *Frame* logo face backwards? You can't answer that either. It just does, because it feels right. If I want something very much, I just do it. I've always dreamed of living on the water. When you're in the water, it's like walking on the moon. You're weightless. Now I'm living in a house I built myself, and it's on a lake. After our children had grown up and left home, my wife and I lived in Cologne for a while. I'm crazy about driving, and Cologne is centrally located, so we drove all over in my Porsche. We went to the Alps and skied – for the first time ever – when we were in our 50s.

Are you inspired by things you see while travelling?
I have a strong interest in new architecture. We've made regular trips specifically to look at certain buildings. I visited Frank Lloyd Wright's house in America, went to Bilbao to see the Guggenheim Museum and to Ronchamp to see Le Corbusier's chapel. I've been to the Vitra Design Museum a couple of times. In my opinion, Frank Gehry is the best architect, bar none. What he does is truly innovative. In the past his designs simply could not have been realized.

But older designs are also fascinating. The idea behind the smoke sauna is 1000 years old, and it still works better than a sauna heated with electricity. And the National Museum is the best museum of Helsinki. I love seeing how our grandparents solved problems. They had to overcome obstacles every day. I do the same thing: solve problems. How can you make what you want to make? That's very interesting.
Can you give me an example? What did you have to solve when designing Dino, for instance?
Dino presented no problems. The design was

THE DOGGY SHELVES, DESIGNED TO STORE CDS, ARE A NEW DESIGN THAT TAKES ITS CUE FROM AARNIO'S DOGGY BUILDING BRICKS.

PUPPY FOR MAGIS IS THE MOST WELL-KNOWN OF AARNIO'S RECENTLY DESIGNED PRODUCTS. PRODUCTION OF THE CANDLEHOLDER ON THE TABLE WAS LIMITED TO A RELATIVELY SMALL NUMBER OF PIECES.

clear from the start. I knew what I wanted to make and how to make it. When I visited the factory to view the prototype, it was exactly as I had thought it would be. The only change I made was to add a bit of clay to make the feet larger. As time goes on, I'm becoming more and more of a sculptor. It's hard to say whether Dino is a design, a sculpture or a chair, but kids really love it.

You've been focusing quite a bit on children lately: Dino for Melaja, Puppy for Magis and Tree for Martela. Why is that?
Eugenio Perazza of Magis came to see me a couple of years ago to ask whether I'd be interested in making something for the Me Too collection. He's a fantastic guy and, like me, a grandfather. It all started with his visit. My grandchildren spend a lot of time with us, and I don't like it when kids do nothing but sit at the computer or watch television. So I make things they can play with or build with, such as my Doggy building blocks. Designing for children is wonderful. It's 'empty'. You can think up whatever you want to. Children will make it work.

What are you working on now?
Right now I'm involved in a project for Alessi. It's great to be designing something small.

I make full-scale drawings of all my designs, so I drew the Ring chair while standing at my desk. Designing for Alessi allows me to work sitting down. I'd also like to design an electric car at some point in the future, but technology is still standing in my way. The battery I'd need for that project currently weighs 500 kg, and the car I have in mind is quite small. Something like the Smart, but a model *so* good that everybody wants one. ▬

eeroaarnio.com

AARNIO'S NEW RING CHAIR IS A CLOSE RELATIVE OF KEINU, HIS ROCKING CHAIR FROM 2002, WHICH HAS CURVED ARMRESTS.

RENDERED IN BLACK AND WHITE, THE MECHANISMS AND FORMS OF EACH PIECE REMAIN THE FOCUS OF THE DESIGN.

A CORD WOVEN THROUGH THE HEM OF THE PUSH LAMP'S 'SKIRT' DIRECTS THE LIGHT.

EXTRACURRICULAR ACTIVITY

Looking for a bit on the side, three KONSTFACK UNIVERSITY students came up with the WHATSWHAT COLLECTIVE.

WORDS **SHONQUIS MORENO**
PHOTOS **STEPHANIE WIEGNER**

Amidst the home décor, the products that looked like other products, and the general lack of vigour that characterized this year's ICFF in New York City, Potential Energy – a lighting presentation tucked into the rear of the Javits Center – made clear that its young designers have, well, a lot of potential. The three sedate lamps on show represented the mostly extracurricular work of three (energetic) Konstfack University students, Englishman John Astbury and Swedes Bengt Brümmer and Karin Wallenbäck, who are currently in their second and final year of the school's MFA programme. The project was initially supervised by professor of industrial design, Teo Enlund, but after dubbing themselves the Whatswhat Collective, the trio brought the debut collection to life in addition to their coursework simply because,

as Astbury puts it, 'We all wanted to do something outside of school, so we started working on this project for ICFF.' In the end, if they were looking for a little extra credit from Professor Enlund, they have certainly earned it.

The Konstfack programme emphasizes discussion and theory alongside product design, and Whatswhat's endeavour represents a valuable practical exercise. Adhering to the notion of potential energy – energy stored within a system thanks to the configuration of its parts – the students produced lamps whose construction suggests latent movement and possible transformation. 'We wanted movement to shift the character of the piece, as well as the light it emits,' Wallenbäck explains. 'Key to all the lamps is how they affect the atmosphere of a room.'

And affect it they do. Adjusting the oversized shade of the Pop desk lamp transforms it from a mood light into a task lamp. The shade of the Pull floor lamp hangs from the light's stem by the slender filament of its partly exposed flex, modestly hinting that the user can move it higher and lower, or into a flexible position (like a torchier), by merely pulling on the flex. Push, a pendant whose shade has the sartorial crispness of an accordion-pleated skirt, can direct light towards the ceiling or floor at the tug of a cord woven through the hem of its 'skirt'.

Not only mechanisms but also materials give the lamps character: sheet plastic laminated with fabric for the shades of the pendant and floor lamps, a plastic (PET) shade and concrete base for the table lamp, and ash for all three. Clean lines, crisp forms and blonde wood ensure a recognizably Scandinavian appearance. 'Tactile qualities were important, as we wanted the lamps to be touched and interacted with,' explains Astbury, 'so we selected materials whose natural properties communicate this message.' Rendered in black and white, the mechanisms and forms of each piece remain the entire focus of the work.

During their summer holiday, the three worked together on a new project. They say it was a combination of naivety and critical analysis that made Potential Energy realize its potential. One hopes the naivety won't wear off too soon. ▰

whatswhatcollective.com

COLLECTION OF LAMPS BY WHATSWHAT. FROM LEFT TO RIGHT: THE POP DESK LAMP, TWO PUSH PENDANTS AND THE PULL FLOOR LAMP.

ADJUSTING THE SHADE OF THE POP DESK LAMP TRANSFORMS IT FROM A MOOD LIGHT INTO A TASK LAMP.

LINES OF VISION

The sole subject of IAN DAVENPORT's work is his medium: paint.

WORDS **LOUISE SCHOUWENBERG, JANE SZITA**
PHOTOS **IAN DAVENPORT, COURTESY OF WADDINGTON GALLERIES LONDON**

Colour, paint and gravity – these are the main ingredients that English abstract artist Ian Davenport (1966) has been using ever since he was a student at Goldsmiths College of Art in London in the 1980s. His paintings and site-specific interventions on the walls of galleries, museums and public buildings never display a single colour but always a fascinating palette of varying colour combinations.

In 1988 he participated in Freeze, a group exhibition curated by Damien Hirst. In 1991 he was nominated for the prestigious Turner Prize. He is represented by Waddington Galleries in London. His paintings have been included in the collections of museums such as Tate Gallery, London; the Weltkunst Collection, Zurich; and the Dallas Museum of Art, Texas.

How did your fascination with paint begin?
As a young boy, I found I could use paint to do things that were quite unexpected. What took a long time was to realize that this could be the subject of my work – that the medium could be the message.

What qualities of paint do you find most intriguing?
I am exploring the organic nature of paint and how it is affected by gravity. Gravity is such a powerful force in our lives and one we take for granted. I am still amazed by the notion that the earth is a big ball spinning through space.

I control fluid paints with minimal interference. I set up a system that enables me to focus on one specific area. At the moment, this system involves putting sequences of coloured, dripped lines together. The way the lines are poured is very precise, even though they

puddle and pool at the bottom. The lines fuse and break in places, but the overall composition is very rhythmic.

You've sometimes used commercial gloss paint. Why?
I wanted to break some rules. At the time, I felt that people seldom questioned how and with what they made paintings. I wanted to examine certain preconceived notions. I thought an interesting way to explore the subject would be to use industrial paints and materials. It led to some very interesting paintings and surfaces, which could not have been made in any other way.

It was also much cheaper to buy large amounts of household paints and lacquers. For an artist just leaving college, this was really important. Over the last 20 years I've used lots of different materials. Most recently I've been using acrylic paints, which I buy from both DIY shops and art suppliers.

What drives your experimentation with different methods of application?
A different method will mean a different set of results. I find the simplest ideas lead to the best results. I have used wind machines, fans, nails, watering cans and syringes to make paintings.

Some of your pieces are prints – are these also an exploration of the paint medium?
I was invited to make prints some years ago. In the beginning, I had no idea how to approach the project. By coincidence I spoke to a friend who explained how I could make an image by working on a clear surface and exposing the result to a light-sensitive screen. From this screen, I can produce a plate for making prints. The different print processes allow me to explore

colour and surface. I find that one medium tends to feed another.

How does an ancient medium like paint retain its relevance in the modern world?
Artists will always find a way of exploring and expressing the world around them. If the approach is relevant, the work will be too.

Where to next with this material?
I want to play with colour. I'm enjoying composing the coloured stripes in my current series of works. Recently I have been using other artists' paintings to influence the colour selection.

Who has influenced your work?
This question follows on very well from the last. Warhol, Matisse, Van Gogh and Fra Angelico have all influenced my work. I am also a big fan of cartoons, like *The Simpsons*. ■

IAN DAVENPORT.
PHOTO MIKE HOBAN

EVERYTHING. PRINT INSTALLATION IN THE DEPARTMENT OF
MATHEMATICS AND STATISTICS AT WARWICK UNIVERSITY.
PHOTO JOHN RIDDY

THE GOSPEL ACCORDING TO JOB

They turn furniture into sculpture, so what would they do with the book? JOB SMEETS, who together with NYNKE TYNAGEL forms STUDIO JOB, talks about the decorative duo's gothic, gilded and gatefolded debut into the world of print.

WORDS **JANE SZITA**

Why did you decide to design *The Book of Job*?
Job Smeets: Back at the end of 2006, Rizzoli invited us to do a book about our work, initially scheduled for release in 2008. As it would be our first book, Nynke [Tynagel] and I thought it made sense to design it ourselves – like two monks. We decided to do one page a day, so as to create an object within our body of work instead of just another book about a design atelier. We wanted something unique that would be available to a select but larger group of people.

Must have been a steep learning curve.
Well, first we had to convince the publisher to work with us in this unorthodox way. Luckily our editor, Ian Luna, and Rizzoli's director, Charles Miers, were both quite progressive and open to new ideas. But it wasn't easy for them or us, since Studio Job had never done a book before and we had to cope with a whole new field – rife with politics, issues and problems. We learned a lot, I can tell you. The concept and creation were completely in our hands, but Rizzoli had the tools and the know-how. They have a great team of professionals and they're tough cookies – but so are we. Fortunately, we had the expertise and coolness of designer Rudo Menge on our side; he's the man responsible for the graphic identity of the Groninger Museum.

Did you approach designing a book differently than designing an object?
It's exactly the same process of creation for us, although books are positioned in a completely different field. It's nice to have gained experience that can be used for future publications. We are already talking with the publisher about an illustrated version of George Orwell's *Animal Farm*, which would be great to do.

Who did what on this project?
Nynke's graphic talent got a lot of attention. She did many new illustrations, graphics and compositions. All brilliant in my opinion. Maybe our next book will be a collection of my drawings. But I'm really hooked on Nynke's work. It's so suitable for this kind of object. My own role was to bring home the content. I invited ten people to write articles for the book. They are all important contributors to the ten-year history of Studio Job: the curator, the gallery owner and so on. I wrote the very personal prologue and epilogue, which are in Dutch – that's why they still rhyme.

You must have put a lot of hours into *The Book of Job*.
More than 1000, but by now we've completely lost count.

At \$150 [approximately €113] a copy, it's something of a design object itself, isn't it?
We felt – and we convinced Rizzoli – that having as much creativity and technique in the book as possible was more important than putting commercial considerations first. We didn't want to publish a standard work in a large edition of 9000 copies, as originally planned. This book is a unique piece published in a limited edition of 3000. The price means you make a conscious decision to buy it or not to buy it. When you do, you have a relevant and durable object to have, to hold, to keep. We wanted to create an object, a collector's item, a cult thing – something without restrictions, relevant enough to purchase in the flesh instead of downloading on your iPad.

So this particular publication won't be available in electronic form then?
Don't know actually. I'm not involved in the sale of the book.

I have heard your book called 'vanity publishing'. What do you have to say to that?
Vanity publishing: that means a book published and financed privately. That's obviously not the case here.

The character of the graphic design seems rooted in the nostalgia of your work.
I don't know why you'd classify our work like that. Studio Job makes objects like a painter does paintings. Would you call a painter 'nostalgic' because he uses paint instead of a printer? When you make objects in small editions, there are certain techniques you use. That has nothing to do with nostalgia. I think it would be good if design [critics] would stop classifying work by the way it's produced. Our work has nothing to do with production techniques of any kind. Our work is about creating an intimate image or moment in a world where everything is mass-related.

But your inspirations – William Blake, illuminated manuscripts – are historical, nevertheless.
And we also looked at ancient books on quackery, alchemy, devil worship and exorcism. Obviously, the Old Testament is an appealing source, too, because of its strange and violent stories, and especially since biblical books are so controversial these days. Angel or devil – it's all the same. Right? ▬

studiojob.be

The Book of Job
Studio Job
Rizzoli New York
ISBN: 978-0-8478-3063-3

20200-MM AND 12200-MM LAMPS.

THIN BLACK LINES

DESIGNER Nendo (nendo.jp)
MATERIAL Steel
COLOUR Black
DIMENSIONS Various
LIMITED EDITION Eight units of each object
PRICE Upon request
GALLERY Phillips de Pury showed the pieces
at the Saatchi Gallery

VASES.

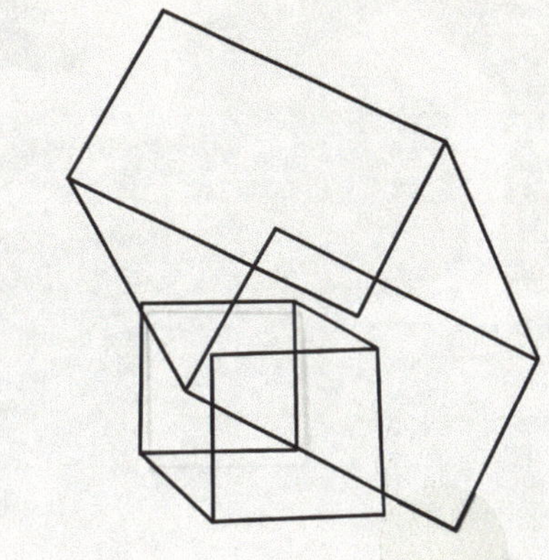
3100-MM CLOCK.

5200-MM STOOL.

WIRED

Scant material and scads of illusion and imagination led NENDO to create the Thin Black Lines collection.

WORDS **FEMKE DE WILD**
PHOTOS **MASAYUKI HAYASHI**

At the Saatchi Gallery in London, Phillips de Pury & Company recently presented Nendo's Thin Black Lines collection. Included are a clock, a stool, tables, mirrors, bowls, lamps and vases, all made from thin solid-steel rods, some angular, some curved. The name of each piece refers to the length of the material used to make it.

Nendo based its latest designs on Japanese calligraphy. These Japanese characters are not elegantly designed letters from an alphabet, however, but abstract drawings pared down to the essence – objects sketched with a brush and black ink. Because each character has a meaning, and because the language is composed of so many characters that a human lifetime is not long enough to learn them all, Japanese calligraphy is seen as a form of art. For Thin Black Lines, Nendo applied the same type of abstraction to interior objects, reducing the designs to an absolute minimum and using thin steel rods to 'sketch', as it were, only the most basic of contours. The objects look quite simple, but the steel has been ingeniously bent to produce a table or a lamp, for instance, in the same way that one stroke of a brush creates a character. The result is a collection that nearly causes the eye to lose sight of the third dimension.

In recent years Nendo has often looked for ways in which to limit materials to a bare minimum. The Cord chair, with its extremely attenuated frame, is a prime example. The original model, which consisted of metal and wood, later evolved into the Wire chair, made completely of metal. In designing the Shortcut towel rack for Boffi, Nendo was clearly well on its way to the Thin Black Lines collection; the same can be said of Roll, designed for Flaminia. But Nendo's latest pieces are not only functional objects crafted from a small amount of material. The lamp resembles a birdcage, the stool could be a drawing by Escher, the clock features an extra dimension rather than a reduction, and Nendo's vase is a metaphor for 'less is more'. It's the combination of a minimum of material and a maximum of illusion and imagination that has gained Nendo's new collection a spot in the much-discussed Saatchi Gallery – and rightly so. ▬

SOCIAL SPHERE BY ELAINE MCLUSKEY AT EDINBURGH NAPIER UNIVERSITY
PHOTO CLAIRE TAYLOR

NIGHT NIGHT LAMP BY VANESSA HORDIES AT ECAL
PHOTO COURTESY OF ECAL

HYLOZOIC GROUND IN VENICE BY PHILIP BEESLEY
PHOTO SERGIO PIRRONE

GALAXY SOHO IN BEIJING BY ZAHA HADID
PHOTO JONATHAN LEIJONHUFVUD

NEXT ISSUE

78

VISIONARY VISTAS

In the next issue of *Frame*, we review the Venice Biennale, and find that visions of beauty have taken the place of architectural theory.
In Beijing, we visit a futuristic Zaha Hadid interior. We meet Didier Faustino, who explores the more enigmatic aspects of built reality, and Erwin Wurm, who playfully distorts the dullest domestic architecture. Finally, we gaze into a crystal ball with the current generation of design students.

AILATI. REFLECTIONS FROM THE FUTURE IN VENICE BY FRANCESCO LIBRIZZI AND SALOTTOBUONO
PHOTO SERGIO PIRRONE